BUSINESS MANAGEMENT AND LEADERSHIP BOOK

Forward:

This book is a study book for anyone interested in finding out how modern business operations work and related business skills you require.

The Book will focus on how to manage or lead a new or existing company which is then managed by the founder or one of the shareholders of the company. This book will also benefit people who work for a company that does not own but runs an organization or business.

First of all, business means buying and selling goods or products that have been traded and exchanged for money. We can say that companies is associated with a business venture by a individuals or organization that has a specific purpose for which the advertiser or a group member has specific interests and goals. This can be either profitable or non-profitable.

There is a need to work on this business, which is called management we can say Management is duties to perform that work.

We can define business management by an organization, which aims to bring people together to demonstrate reaching the desired goals and special education, which is used as resources to benefit the organization.

We regard the business as a well organized support system with a framework for action. We can define the Management is the human behavior of doing work such as planning and executing the work, organizing and stopping so that it can operate as a productive system. The work that is being done is either allocated someone or sending a group of people to perform it.

It is better to say that business is all about the growth of a business and the sources of production that generate profits that are related to whether it sells or provides a service whether it is profitable or not.

They point out that business is all about the growth of a business and the sources of profit that are sold or provided for a service whether it is profitable or not.

The word management is an English word originating from the 15th century French word Mesnager which is used in the language of the horse, which means to hold the horse in hand, and the Spanish word Mesnager means to be controlled horses which later became the English language in the 17th and 18th centuries and became the current language of management.

Entrepreneurship is created when the needs and aspirations of people, organizations and government customers in the market are realized.

Business management is the management, coordination and organization of business activities, including the supply of materials, resources and machinery, which deals with innovation, production and marketing.

In other words management work I can say is the responsibility of planning, organizing, directing and protecting revenue sources to achieve the goals of economic growth.

Management functions include the following:
• Organization
• Leadership
• Planning
• Staffing
• Organization control

Management also includes transformation, and the exchange of resources, natural resources, manpower and existing technology resources. Managing a business facilitates a joint effort and effort to achieve the company's goals.

Abdi abdillahi Hassan[mattan]

Introduction:

Working on business management can be exciting, but it can also create new challenges. Although management requires knowledge and experience in which certain skills can be learned or gained, there are no specific skills or techniques you can learn to become an excellent manager, however in this book you can find more information, tips for managing a business or organization you need. As a result, you can lead your business or team to greater growth and greater productivity.

Business management is an important issue, both in terms of business operations and personnel management. I tried to start at the beginning of each chapter with the types of business management. I will then first give the definition and theory on the subject then being discussed.

There are also examples and guides in some areas regarding business management and how it works. We will also look at the topics covered in this book in a local and international format, as well as the pros and cons of the topic. We conclude each chapter with suggestions and recommendations on this topic.

The book is written in a good format, and is divided into 9 Units in a row, each chapter consisting of six to seven different articles, all of which deal with the management and leadership required of an organization existing business.

Chapter one:

Business management, we focus on: Introduction to business management, Business objectives, Business management components, Business management Pros and Cons, International Marketing, and will conclude with Recommendation and suggestions.

Chapter two:

Chapter two is about Business leadership. We focus on, Differences between Leader and Manager, Introduction to business leadership, Leadership theory, Leadership styles, Leadership Theory, Business management and leadership Pros and cons, Suggestions how to improve business leadership.

Chapter three:
Marketing Management, Customer Target Marketing Strategies, Scope of Marketing, Marketing Strategies, Marketing Objectives, Marketing management functions, Development of Marketing Concept, Marketing values, Understanding customer needs, wants and demand, The five key product levels are, Marketing Mix, International marketing

Chapter Four

Consumer behavior, Introduction consumer behavior, Customer orientation, Analysis of Consumers behavior, How Consumers behavior applies to reality, Conclusion, Suggestion and Recommendations,

Chapter Five:

Human Resources Management, Introduction HRM,Back ground history, Current Human Resources Management, Functions of the HRM department, HRM objectives Present and Current of HR situation, Pros and Cons HRM management, Summery and conclusions, Recommendations.

Chapter SIX

Operational Management, What operational management, Production management------------- Trending production management, Operation management linked market competition, How to get the most out of market competition, Operational strategy, Pros and Cons operational management, Conclusion: How to improve operation management, Recommendations

Chapter seven:

This chapter highlightes Financial management, Financial management in business,Financial management Concept,Objectives of Finance management, Capital Markets, Financial management and its functions,Advantage and disadvantage of financial management, International financial management,Recommendation how to improve financial management.

Chapter Eight:

Business policies, Introduction to Business Policies,Objectives for Business policy and strategy course,General Analysis about the Business policy and strategy, Features of Strategies,How business strategy topic applies to reality, Developing a Business Strategy, Discussions Pros and cons on Business strategy, Suggestion and Recommendations

Chapter Nine

This chapter explores Business Communication Introduction to Business communication, Types of communication, General Analysis about the Business communication, How business communication applies to reality, Components of communication, Pros and cons of the topic ,Recommendations and suggestions, Conclusions

Acknowledgments:

I would like to thank the people who inspired me to write this book, first and foremost my wife Ilhan Abdirahman Ibrahim, My niece Saynab Mohamed Abdillahi who edited the book, and my lectureres in Atlantic Unversity I would also like to thank everyone who contributed to the production and publication of this book.

Dedication:
I dedicate this book to my parents, my father Abdillahi Hassan Matan, and my mother Ebado Esse Egeh. They are both dead, I pray to God to shower His mercy on them and on Muslims. I would also like to dedicate to all my brothers, uncles (ANJHKW), aunts, uncles and a large family of Hassan Matan.

BIOGRAPHY OF THE AUTHOR

Dr. Abdi Abdillahi Hassan Matan was born in 1965 in the village of Haydh Ducato in the Togdheer region. The first kindergarten he entered was in 1972, which was the Macalim Qasim Madarass in Burao.
In 1975 he was enrolled in the November 21 primary school in Burao(Qasabka), and in 1981 he graduated from Mohamud Ahmed Mohamed Ali Middle School. In 1985 he graduated from Sheikh Bashir Secondary School.

In 1986 the author was one of the students who joined the Somali National Movement (SNM). He was part of the Liberation Army that entered Burao on 27 May 1988, where he was wounded.

Dr. Hassan left the country in 1989 for the Netherlands, where he lived for a long time and continued his further education.

In 1995 he completed his college education and majored in social studies with a Diploma. In 2001 he graduated from an applied science university in the Netherlands, studied social sciences, and received a bachelor's degree in Social Science.

In 2005 Dr. Hassan received a Master's degree from a University in London and further developed his studies in development and social Science.

He also took a post graduate course in economics from the University of Hollowing in London. In 2021, Abdi completed his PhD, graduating from a university in the United States with a degree in International Business Administration.

Dr. Hassan has held various positions in various countries such as the Netherlands as a social worker, and has worked with the local, central government of the Netherlands and voluntary organizations.

Dr. Hassan also worked for the London Brough of Greenwich as a Social Worker. During his stay in the diaspora, he was one of the most active members of the Somaliland Diaspora community, and was an active member of the Somaliland Diaspora organisations.

The author returned to Somaliland in late 2010 and began his first career in Somaliland with the Civil Service Commission, a former secretary of the Civil Service Reform Commission.

In 2011 Dr. Hassan moved to the Ministry of Labor and Social Affairs and became the head of child protection in Somaliland, and in 2012 he was appointed Director of the Department of Social Affairs. In 2016 he moved to SOS International and became the Head of Child Protection in Somalia and Somaliland.

In mid-2016, Dr. Hassan was appointed by then-President Ahmed Mohamed Silanyo as the Deputy General Manager of the Berbera Port, which later became the Somaliland Ports Authority.

In 2020 – Dr. Hassan is currently the advisor to the Minister of Parliamentary Relations and Constitutional Affairs in Somaliland.

In addition, Dr. Hassan, a Somaliland scholar, has taught at various universities and colleges, including, Admass University, Golis University, and the Civil Service Institute in Hargeisa.

He is interested in and writes on socio-economic, cultural, social and political developments in Somalia and the Horn of Africa and beyond. He wrote also different books in different topic in both Somali and English.

Dr. Hassan also believes in the idea of Pan Africanism, and the idea of globalization.

Dr. Hassan is encouraging democratization process in the horn of Africa. He is member of human rights activist organizations and he works to create and maintain peace and stability in the Horn of Africa

He is also peace creator and human rights activist.

Sidiq aw Farah Gabar
Somaliland writer, journalist and poet.

Table of contents:

Chapter Three:

3. Marketing Management,

Chapter Four

CHAPTER FIVE:

Chapter SIX

Chapter 7:

Chapter 8

Chapter Nine

Chapter one:

1.   Business management:

1.1   Introduction to Business management

First of all, business means buying and selling goods or products that have been traded and exchanged for money. We can say that a business is associated with a business venture by a individuals or organization that has a specific purpose for which the advertiser or a group member has specific interests and goals. This can be either profitable or non-profitable.

There is a need to work on this business, which is called management, we can say the Management is to perform that work.

We can define business management by an organization, which aims to bring people together to demonstrate reaching the desired goals and special education, which is used as resources to benefit the organization.

We regard the business as a well organized support system with a framework for action. Management could be defined is the human behavior of doing work such as planning and executing the work, organizing and stopping so that it can operate as a productive system. The work that is being done is either allocated someone or sending a group of people to perform it.

It is better to say that business is all about the growth of a business and the sources of production that generate profits that are related to whether it sells or provides a service whether it is profitable or not.

They point out that business is all about the growth of a business and the sources of profit that are sold or provided for a service whether it is profitable or not.

Mintzberg, H.(2014). The word management is an English word originating from the 15th century French word Mesnager which is used in the language of the horse, which means to hold the horse in hand, and the Spanish word Mesnager means to be controlled horses which later

12

became the English language in the 17th and 18th centuries and became the current language of management.

Entrepreneurship is created when the needs and aspirations of people, organizations and government customers in the market are realized.

Different scholars have given different views and definitions to the management which are:

Henri Fayol (1841-1925) said: "Management is planning and vision, management, command, coordination and control.

Fredmund Malik (1944-) described management as "changes in the use of resources Management is the coordination and use of all production tools and equipment including machinery, equipment, human resources and finances.

Ghislain Deslandes defines management as "a weak force, a pressure to achieve results and a given triangular power of restraint, modeling and imagination, operating at individual, institutional levels and environment".

Peter Drucker (1909-2005) saw the basic function of management as two factors: marketing and creativity. However, creativity is also linked to marketing (product innovation is central to strategic marketing, business management knowledge.

We can also say that managing a number of complex tasks such as setting up a strategy for a company or organization and staffing using available resources such as money, natural resources, technology and personnel is required, which is to balance market fluctuations in products and market demands based on existing customer needs in the market.

Managing requires knowledge, competence, perseverance and consistent decision-making. Then you study at colleges and universities with various specializations such as diploma, bachelor's degree, and master's degree or PhD degrees.

1.2. Business Objectives:

Businesses should have a set of goals they want to achieve. In general, business companies have the following objectives.
I. To efficiently and effectively produce products or provide services to meet the needs and demands of users in the market.
ii. To generate enough income to make a profit.
iii. To protect the well-being of employees. To achieve this, personnel management and labor relations are needed. NS. Ensure good social relations with plant neighbors and citizens.

v. To do this, the company may make special social obligations, such as providing access to roads, drinking water and scholarship awards to eligible students, farm neighbors or working children.

1.3. General Analysis about the Business Management

Business management is the management, coordination and organization of business activities, including the supply of materials, resources and machinery, which deals with innovation, production and marketing.

In other words management work I can say is the responsibility of planning, organizing, directing and protecting revenue sources to achieve the goals of economic growth.

Dubrin, Andrew J. (2009). Most companies and corporations have three hierarchical structures that are structured like a pyramid structure as follows:

The top executives of the company, who lead the company as members of the board of directors and the CEO. They set the policies and strategies for running the business. They also decide on the overall structure of the organization or company.

Senior managers are usually people who are knowledgeable and skilled in business management, are responsible for leading and directing the central management of an organization or company, and have open communication with the middle management and the senior management of the company that owns or manages.

Middle Managers: The middle managers are the heads of the middle administration and especially the managers of the departments or branches of an organization or company, the managers of the regions, and the managers of the divisions according to the companies or organizations structure.

Middle managers also guide and provide frontline managers. Intermediate managers direct and communicate to the subordinate management the policies and strategies from the top management of the company. Subordinate managers: Subordinate managers are the ones who oversee the workplace and the frontline executives, who provide instructions, advice and how to do the job.

These three components of a company are chain management must communicate these three levels of trust and co-operation in order for the organization or organization to achieve its goals.

The CEO and managers of the companies have the responsibility to manage and ensure the smooth running of the business activities in the area and the decisions that are required to be made there. Management is everything related to business from the number of one or more people to a large population or organization to a thousand people in different cities and countries.

The policy is defined by the company's board of directors and is enforced by general managers and subordinates.

It is possible to assess the future of the company and the value it will then have depending on the knowledge, experience and quality of the managers of the company.

Management functions include the following:
• Organization
• Leadership
• Planning
• Staffing
• Organization control

Management also includes transformation, and the exchange of resources, natural resources, manpower and existing technology resources. Managing a business facilitates a joint effort and effort to achieve the company's goals.

1.4 What is a Business Management System?

Business Management System is a tool used to implement the planning and strategic planning of business processes, structures, and policies, procedures to deliver, implement, and develop business strategies and plans, as well as everything related to business management activities.

Provides strategic and tactics business decisions when it comes to current processes, work and implementation that address the overall specific goals of the organization or company depending on meeting the expectations and needs of the customers.

The key objective of the Business Management System is to provide management with the tools to monitor, plan, and control their activities and measure business performance.

They also aim to implement a system that promotes sustainable growth. This management approach conveys the principles of company sustainability and has an impact on the overall roadmap of a company business.

These lead to different levels depending on how the for profit organization or company will perform the various tasks required of it, including recruitment, marketing, sales, and acquisition to achieve its goals

High and Low Value Strategies

The strategy is not to always go cheap or low price but to get a cheap product, but that is the clear path. Some strategies are tactically expensive, by measuring our psychological desire to measure the high quality of a high cost product.

Other strategies that can lower the sale price of an inexpensive investment and pay off time are up to 30 days and up to one year.

1.5 Business management Components:

1.5.1 Marketing Management

Marketing management is the organizational behavior of a company in which organizations or companies study how best to get their business to market and how best to conduct marketing orientation, most relevant messages and media resources to find out and monitor and respond to market customers' responses.

Marketing management also helps the company operate the financial resources and create a competitive strategy to discuss the formal business model of the company.

Marketing managment we will discuss in detail in chapter 5

1.5.2   Human Resources Management(HRM)

HRM is the study of activities related to the people working in the organization. It is the responsibility of the administration to work to meet the needs of the organization in terms of the skills and abilities of the employees.

We can define HRM as the management of recruitment and promotion and care for the people working in the organization and the workforce focuses on the employees working in the organization.

HRM was established as a management system to ensure that human talent is used, efficiently and effectively to achieve the organization's goals.

In other words, HRM is a staff office responsible for recruiting, developing, compensating, integrating and caring for the organization's staff, which aims to help the organization achieve its specific goals.

Human Resources Managment would be discussed in detail in chapter 5

1.5.3   What is Operational Management?

Investopia(2019) Operational management can be defined as the management of business behaviors to create the most effective and efficient production within the organization or company, and is related to the conversion of goods and other business services into more efficient and effective services, possible to then increase the company's productivity.

Operational management is the process of managing the design and control of the production process and restructuring the business operations of a product or service.

Performance management also involves the acquisition of manpower, technology, and systems within a company with the necessary experiences and capabilities related to the delivery of the organization's goods or services.

This part of the operation also manages the direct routes that are necessary for the company to produce and then access the products and services provided by the company.

The operational unit also works to learn the behaviors and skills in the designing, planning, and implementation of production systems and processes to achieve organizational goals.

Operational Managment would be discussed in detail in chapter 6

1.5.4 Financial management

Finance can be defined as managing, creating and analyzing money and investments. It focuses on finding answers to questions related to how a person, company or government makes money, which we know as capital in terms of business, and how that money is used or invested. . Finance has different components such as: private finance, corporate finance and public finance.

Investing is also about ensuring that money flows easily and securely through the business, which can then be achieved by strengthening investments and deploying other financial resources.

Finance, therefore, refers to the study of securities. Securities are financial instruments that can be purchased and used to accumulate capital in public and private markets.

Financial Managment would be discussed in detail in chapter 7.

1.6 What is a Business Model?

The business model is the company's plan to get the fruit or make a profit. After research it presents the products or services of the business that are ready to be sold, the market focus that is allocated, and the expected costs for it.

Planning and choosing this type of business is important for both new and existing businesses. It helps new comers to the market to invest in business development, and inspires and motivates the company's management and staff.

Existing businesses need to constantly review and update their business plans otherwise they will not be able to successfully anticipate future trends and challenges, which is critical to the success of that business.

Business plans make it easier for investment companies to evaluate companies that are interested in investing.

Taking the Key the format Entrepreneurship is an important strategy a for profit company to make a successful business. We can specify information about the goods or services that the business plans to sell, the markets targeted, and the costs expected to be used.

The two business levers of the business model are cost and expense. So when the investor is evaluating the business model it is worth looking at or asking the entrepreneur what the business idea is doing and the cost as well as the cost.

Fayol 14 principles of Management

Henry Fayol the father of modern management came up with new ideas for the concept of management. This provides a comprehensive overview that can be used at different levels of governance and management. Fayol concepts are used by managers of various organizations to manage the internal workings of the organization.

Fayo explained enabling administrative transparency. We have developed the 14 governing principles which are detailed below:

Fayo focused on achieving administrative transparency. The fourteen principles of governance created by Henri Fayol are explained below.

1. Distribution of Work

Mr. Fayol believed that sorting and distributing work could help increase productivity and the quality of a variety of products. It can also help ensure that the job is done correctly and efficiently and that the staff performs the job responsibly. The principle of division of labor is good for both managers and the lower level of the technical team doing the work.

2. Power and Responsibility

In the case of management it is important to pay special attention to the powers and responsibilities, which enable the administration to carry out its duties efficiently and effectively, and the responsibility leads to the person being responsible to capture or lead to capture and assign to the perpetrator.

3. Ethics

Discipline is important to the values or essentials of any project or administration. The positive results of the work done and the effective relationships made make it easier to get the job done and carried out as intended.

Good manners and attitudes also make it easier for employees to grow well and make significant progress in their careers.

4. Unity of Command-

It means that the staff has only one boss or manager to follow and carry out his orders, if the staff orders more than one supervisor it can lead to conflict and confusion resulting in conflicting interests of the leader.

5. Unity of Directions

Each person or group working together should have a common goal, which can be achieved by everyone who works for a company and has the sole purpose of participating and working for the organization or company to achieve the goal, which makes the work easier to achieve her successful goal.

6. Reducing Personal Interests

Reducing personal interests and working for the common good of the company or organization, and it is forbidden for personal and company interests to clash and each employee must work for the interests and goals of the organization or company. That is why the general goal of a company is to put your personal interests ahead of those of an organization or company. This is what guides the company's hierarchy and orders

7. The allowance

It is important that the company's employees are encouraged to do the job honestly; the salary can be cash or non-cash. In any case, the salary should be a reward for the hard work of the company's employees.

8. Centralization

Managers and other company executives responsible for participating in decision-making should be neutral, depending on the size and scope of the company. Fayo says there is a balance between hierarchy and division of power.

9. Scalar chain

Fayol refers to the principle that the hierarchy should be from top to bottom, and it is important for each employee to know who is the closest boss, and it is also important that they are able to communicate, can each of their leaders when needed take into account the hierarchy.

10. Order

It is also important that the company maintains an existing working order, so that it has a good work ethics. Productivity is influenced by the current working environment. Positive work environment leads to productivity growth.

11. Equality

One of the basic principles of the company is to treat employees fairly with respect and dignity, and it is one of the job responsibilities of the person in charge or manager not to discriminate against them at work.

12. Stability

Workers do their job well and efficiently if they feel safe and secure at work. Management must work to ensure that workers are safe to carry out their work without fear of reprisals and to ensure the safety and well-being of employees.

It is the duty of management to provide occupational safety to their employees.

13. Initiative
The manager also helps and encourages the staff to come up with new ideas and suggestions, in order to find organizational activities, which in turn can increase the employee's interest in the work and also feel valued.

14. Esprit de Corps

It is also important that the authorities encourage them to support each other at all times, and that building trust and understanding can lead to better results and a better working environment.

Finally the 14 Principles of Management are used to manage an organization and are useful for predicting, planning, decision making, organizing and managing the process, controlling and coordinating work.

1.6 Business management Pros and cons of on a local, national and international level

Prosancons(2018) Business management is related to managing and managing a business whether it is a private business owned by you, or one you manage it. It has many benefits that cannot be summed up. To be successful in this business you need to have the knowledge, ability and experience to run the business.

So business management has both advantages and disadvantages. I would like to point out first of all the advantages of business management here:

1.6.1 Pros

1. Windstorming: Business management brings many benefits, which allows an entrepreneur to make more money quickly, than you would if you were an employee working for someone else.

2. Independence: You become an independent person, who makes all the important decisions without consulting anyone and without wasting time consulting anyone.

3. When you become a business manager, you will have the opportunity to create jobs by hiring other professionals who contribute to the local economy in which the business or company operates. As a result, the people you employ can make a difference in their lives.
4. Safety: Business managers and owners maintain security during working hours and are not afraid of being fired.
5. Discovery: Business managers have their own ideas that they want to implement, in which you decide which ideas you can apply and which ones will not work for the business.

6. Oversight: The business manager has the final control over the business and you can make your own decisions, without having to consult with anyone else.

7. Experience: You have the opportunity to learn about every aspect of business, and always learn something new, which enhances the knowledge and experience of the person who runs the business.

8. Communication: you work directly with your customer, and provide for their needs, resulting in the creation of a personal relationship between the manager and his clients.

9. Self-confidence: can create an environment of personal satisfaction based on a successful business, which can lead to personal confidence that you can do more.

10. Interest: you get the chance to really work at your favorite place, or you prefer to work there, which you do every day for pleasure.

11. Long-term: You can also make plans to retire, which you have enough money to live on.

12. Creating: Business management helps you to have better relationships with the community and to have a sense of belonging and stability.

1.6.2 Cons:

1. Funding: If you fail in this business financing process, you run the risk of becoming an unrecognized financial risk.

2. Ill health: In business you are likely to work long hours, not having time to take vacations which can have long-term health effects.

3. time consume: Entrepreneurship requires you to spend a lot of time, which is seen as wasting your time doing the things you love to do. This can eventually lead to a lot of interest in the job that you are not enjoying.

4. Inconsistency: Your income may fluctuate and sometimes your income is very low, and there may be uncertainty about your income.

5. Persecution: You may have to make difficult decisions and later resent yourself such as someone you fired, a friend you refused to hire, which can lead to personal pressure and thoughtfulness, Which can affect your relationships with others.

6. Learning: you may need to increase your knowledge such as filing and accounting, inventory control, planning, advertising, market research and general business management issues.

7. Legal loans: You should be careful to keep and comply with all the rules, and you should be careful about lawsuits that customers or employees may sue you for.

8. Restrictions: Your time is limited and you may not be able to do many things you used to be able to do before becoming a business manager.

9. Always watched: you are monitored, you are not free to do anything or anything special, and your actions may have a special impact on you and your business.

10. Long Wait Results: Sometimes it takes a long time to make a profit from your business and successes you want to achieve with your business.

1.7 International Marketing:

In international marketing we mean marketing doing business outside the borders of the country or abroad,and there are many companies that operate and export goods and services around the world, which in turn facilitates the growth of foreign exchange.

While international marketing can be profitable, these companies may also face legal challenges from their overseas counterparts, which international companies are trying to find solutions to overcome through the World Trade Organization?

But it is better for international companies that want to operate in foreign countries to do market research before starting a business which can give a better view of the market in which they are investing or operating with a focus on people, their culture, their needs, etc., which the companies themselves can do research on, or they can hire another company to do the research.

1.7.1 Advantages of international marketing:

1. Costs:

If a company increases the number of products it sells in the international markets it operates in, it will increase revenue and profit and reduce its costs. Companies operating in international markets are also gaining traction in local and international markets or in other countries in which they operate.
.

2.   Can deal with seasonal changes:

Clothing manufacturers such as summer period, which operate in colder climates, are required for a limited period of time if they are limited to markets only such as these cold European ones in the United States.

And these companies need to take their clothes to other global markets with warmer climates so that they can meet the needs of those markets and find a market to sell their products.

3. Increases profits:

As companies increase market demand for their products, productivity and revenue also increase, making the company more competitive in the business market, as well as generating more revenue and profits.
.

4. Receives foreign exchange:
Overseas companies help the company to find a foreign exchange in the country that is beneficial for the foreign exchange market.

5. Employment: Companies operating in international trade create jobs in their home country and those of other host countries.

Disadvantages of international marketing:

1. Multiculturalism: There may be differences in the culture of the company of origin and the cultures of the countries in which the company operates, and these different cultures may clash.

2. War: In the event of war or instability in the host countries, this may result in loss to the company.

3. Infrastructure: Infrastructure in host countries, especially developing countries, most of them are less developed and compatible with international ones.

4. Government regulations: Laws and regulations in the host countries can be a barrier to foreign companies entering and investing in the country, as they compete with local businesses. Hosts can also put pressure on their governments not to import workers but to employ them.

5. Integrated Marketing: Business companies operating overseas may engage in integrated marketing of products in the host country rather than in the home country which may incur additional costs.

1.8 Recommendation and suggestions:

When you run a business, whether you own a business or not, you need to develop your business so that you can be a successful entrepreneur in the open competitive market. It is not limited to the home country, but you can get big pictire, well-known companies with strong financial and marketing capabilities that can take your business out of business even if your business is small and is still growing.

You are also in competition with companies operating in locally or in your home country, which are competing with businesses that may be financially and politically more powerful than you, which require you to think about and make a policy and a clear business strategy so that you can achieve your business goals now, in the near future or in the long term future.

In order to adapt to changing trends and situations you need to be proactive in adapting to new emerging circumstances, and you can experiment with new and more appropriate ways for your business to work best.

In order to adapt to these issues you need to take appropriate action, the most effective ways of changing the business environment is to look at and conduct research how successful businesses work and the steps they have taken that have led to their success.

You can also compare different companies in or near your business type and then evaluate that company to get a better idea of what to get from each one, and then pick the one that you think is most effective most likely to benefit your business.

It is also a good idea to take advantage of the personal experience of the business, and also strive to update their knowledge and skills in business management because the world is changing, and business is one of the things you change with the economy and productivity.

It is also important to keep abreast of the relevant business market and the ever-changing developments that you must keep up with. To achieve this objective you need to conduct regular market research studies related to marketing in your field.

 In addition to promoting new business ideas and perspectives and innovations, the use of new tools and systems such as IT and advertising for the continued use of social media and social media.

1.8.1 The following best practice business strategy can help your business:

- Be prepared to compete in the commercial market as well as compete for tangible success.
- Increase sales and access to new commercial markets
- Reduce and significantly reduce company costs.
- The employees of the company to be active and efficient, as well as to increase the workforce
- Effective use of technology.
- To clean up and reduce waste and improve quality
- Respond quickly to creativity in your work or business segment

1.8.2 The best management methods include:

- That the company has a communication system with clear goals and strategies to utilize it.
- The company manager should be a leader who sets a good example for the employees.
- Setting needs that required to be met and reasonable
- An open management system based on dialogue and persuasion
- Develop a clear and careful strategic plan.

There are also business tools that can be used to achieve the best management system including:

- Compare your company or business with benchmarking
- Forecasting: forecasting company productivity and economic growth in the near future, and finding new markets
- financial planning: production and revenue, expenses and debt of the company and how to find a balance between them.

- Strategic planning: Have a clear business strategic plan and how to succeed in the business market
- Performance monitoring: to keep abreast of developments by constantly monitoring and evaluating the company's performance and achieving its goals.

1.9 Conclusion

The business as a well organized support system with a framework for action. Management we can define is the human behavior of doing work such as planning and executing the work, organizing and stopping so that it can produce a productive system. The work that is being done is either allocated someone or sending a group of people to perform

Management functions include the following:
• Organization
• Leadership
• Planning
• Staffing
• Organization control

When you run a business, whether you own a business or not, you need to develop your business so that you can be a successful entrepreneur in the open competitive market. It is not limited to the home country, but you can get big picture marketing strategy , well-known companies with strong financial and marketing capabilities that can take your business out of business even if your business is small and we are still growing.

You are also in competition with companies operating in locally or your home country, which are competing with businesses that may be financially and politically more powerful than you, which you require to think about and make a policy and a clear business strategy so that you can achieve your business goals now, in the near future or in the long term future.

Business management is related to adminstration and managing a business whether it is a private business owned by you, or one you manage it. It has many benefits that cannot be summed up. To be successful in this business you need to have the knowledge, ability and experience to run the business.
So business management has both advantages and disadvantages.

If a company increases the number of products it sells in the international markets it operates in, it will increase revenue and profit and reduce its costs. Companies operating in international markets are also gaining traction in local and international markets or in other countries in which they operate in.

1.11 Refrencies

Deslandes G., (2014), "Management in Xenophon's Philosophy : a Retrospective Analysis", 38th Annual Research Conference, Philosophy of Management, 2014, July 14–16, Chicago

Dubrin, Andrew J. (2009). *Essentials of management (8th ed.). Mason, OH: Thomson Business & Economics. ISBN 978-0-324-35389-1. OCLC 227205643.*

Frank, Prabbal (2007). *People Manipulation: A Positive Approach (2 ed.). New Delhi: Sterling Publishers Pvt. Ltd (published 2009). pp. 3–7. ISBN 978-81-207-4352-6. Retrieved 2015-09-05. There is a difference*

Harper, Douglas. *"management". Online Etymology Dictionary. Retrieved 2015-08-29.* – "Meaning 'governing body' (originally of a theater) is from 1739

Investopia(2019, onlineavailable: https://www.investopedia.com/terms/o/operations-management.asp, retrieved on 25/11/2021

Gulshan, S. *Management Principles and Practices by Lallan Prasad and SS Gulshan. Excel Books India. pp. 6–. ISBN 978-93-5062-099-1*

Langfred, Claus (2000). *"The paradox of self-management: individual and group autonomy in work groups". Journal of Organizational Behavior. 21 (5): 563–585. doi:10.1002/1099-1379(200008)21:5<563::AID-JOB31>3.0.CO;2-H.*

Lumineau, Fabrice; Oliveira, Nuno (2017). *"A Pluralistic Perspective to Overcome Major Blind Spots in Research on Interorganizational Relationships". Academy of Management Annals*

Powell, Thomas C. (2001). *"Competitive advantage: logical and philosophical considerations". Strategic Management Journal. 22 (9): 875–888. doi:10.1002/smj.173. ISSN 1097-0266.*

Mintzberg, H.(2014). *Manager l'essentiel : ce que font vraiment les managers ... et ce qu'ils pourraient faire mieux. Paris: Vuibert*

Powell, Thomas C. (2001). *"Competitive advantage: logical and philosophical considerations". Strategic Management Journal. 22 (9): 875–888. doi:10.1002/smj.173. ISSN 1097-0266.*

Langfred, Claus (2000). *"The paradox of self-management: individual and group autonomy in work groups". Journal of Organizational Behavior. 21 (5): 563–585. doi:10.1002/1099-1379(200008)21:5<563::AID-JOB31>3.0.CO;2-H.*

Lumineau, Fabrice; Oliveira, Nuno (2017). *"A Pluralistic Perspective to Overcome Major Blind Spots in Research on Interorganizational Relationships". Academy of Management Annals*

*Wood, Robert; Bandura, Albert (1989). "Social Cognitive Theory of Organizational Management". The Academy of Management Review. **14** (3): 361–384. doi:10.2307/258173. ISSN 0363-7425. JSTOR 258173.*

CHAPTER TWO

2   Business Leadership:

2.1 Differences between Leader and Manager:

We talked about Business management in the first chapter, and in this second chapter we will discussed about Business leader.

People are often confused by the leadership and the managment of the organisation, and many people think they are the same, so there are a lot of things that they can have in common, but they are still very different, the leader of the people follows and supports, while and the manager engages the people and works well with them.

The leader encourages people to better understand and be satisfied with the goals of the company and that the employees then work with them to achieve the goals of the company or organization.

Where the manager is the one who is overworked and manages the work to be done and the day-to-day tasks to be carried out as intended and carried out as intended.

And small companies need to be both strong leaders and managers so that people can come down and convince them to work on their vision to achieve success.

Then each organization must be clear that there is a leader and a manager or that there is a leader and a manager who is in charge of the two activities, and both of them are inextricably linked, and each one's role is clear. Attempting to separate can lead to more challenges than a solution can.

Then every organization and company needs to have management that can plan, organize, coordinate staff, and an inspiring and motivated leader to achieve the desired goal.

Leaders often believe that the success of the organization is made possible by the people or employees of the organization, and praise the success of the people who lead it.

While many managers are focused, they are aware of the mistakes and weaknesses of people and may not have the wrong motive but want to correct them.

Successful leaders present their vision of the company's potential, and strive to inspire and engage their people to make that vision truly successful.

The business leader has a good understanding of how high-level teams can do the job, much more when they work together to do a better job rather than individual employees, which in turn encourages them to take the initiative come to a team that works together confidently and does the work together.

In other words, it is not necessary for the leader and the manager to be two **separate individuals and the person with the above view can do the job well** in both roles.

Managers, focus on setting, measuring and achieving goals by checking and controlling situations to achieve their goals.

Mean while I would discuss in this chapter effective leadership in the organization. I would focus the following topics:

2.1.2 Leadership
- Leadership definition and introduction of the leadership.
- Leadership theory
- Leadership styles
- Personal development

2.2 Introduction business leadership

Leadership is defined as "a process of social influence in which one person can receive the help and support of others to achieve a specific goaL, and there are other definitions of leadership. For example, some understand a leader as simpler as a person earns the respect and trust of others who accept to follow his or her advice or instructions, who guide or guide others, while others interpret leadership as organizing and directing a group of people to achieve a common goal.

Leadership is the process of gaining the influence by giving people clear goals, direction, and inspiration while working on achieving the goal and mission of the organization(Reimer, 2006).

To make clear the definition and the topic, I will discuss the following influence, purpose and vision, motivation, and improving which are factors important for the context of leadership.

2.2.1 Influence:

The influence will force people or staff, and national and international partners - to do what is necessary for the task at hand. The effect is stronger than the orders given, and it allows for better decision-making without any pressure.

The examples taken by the individual leader are better and more important than the verbal cues. Leaders are examples of people below them, good and bad in the workplace, every action they take or every statement they make while at work or absent from work. Through personal words and examples, leaders communicate purpose, direction, and motivation. (Reimer, 2006).

2.2.2. Purpose and vision:

Purpose gives leaders followers stimulate to take an action in order to achieve the desired result. Leaders must give a clear purpose to their supporters or subordinates and do it in different ways. Leaders can use direct communication to achieve their goals through requests or instructions on what to do. Vision is another way leaders can communicate their purpose.

Goal refers to an organized goal that may be larger or less influential than other objectives. Top leaders carefully consider how to present their own point of view.

Providing a clear direction involves communicating how to achieve the goal: prioritizing tasks, assigning responsibilities for completion, and making sure those below them understand the way the work is to be done. While subordinates want and need guidance, they expect hard work, quality training, and adequate resources.

Appropriate freedom of action must be provided. Providing a clear direction allows those who follow the freedom to change plans and orders to adapt to changing circumstances. Orientation while adapting to change is a constant process.

Although many leaders are tired of hearing from the officer about how well they are doing and that they are important in achieving the goal, they know it is true and appreciate the comments. Each time a senior managers submits information during a meeting, he sends a clear indication: people are being cared for and valued. The subordinates will do their jobs well because they earned their leaders trust.

2.2.3 Motivation:

Motivation provides the desire to do what is necessary to achieve a goal. Motivation comes from within, but it is influenced by the actions and words of others. The role of the leader in motivation is to understand the needs and wants of others, to adapt and promote the driving individuals of the team's goals, and to influence others to achieve those great goals. Some people have a high level of motivation to do the job, while others need more confidence and feedback.

Motivation encourages effort when something needs to be completed. As a leader, most likely familiar with the capabilities and limitations of others, and then take responsibility for most you can.

2.2.4 Improving:

Improving the future means capturing and practicing important lessons that are ongoing and completing projects and operations. After inspection to ensure that all equipment has been repaired, cleaned, accounted for, and properly disassembled is a scientific discussion of an event, focused on performance levels. It allows participants to find out what happened, why it happened, how to maintain strengths, and how to develop weaknesses.

Taking advantage of honest feedback, the leader points out areas of error or oil, to maintain identification of areas of strength and weaknesses to improve the situation there. If it is proven that team members have spent too much time on certain tasks while neglecting others, the leader may improve the process or advise specific people on how to do better.

Development counseling is important to help people below them improve performance and prepare for future responsibilities. Counseling should address the strengths as well as the weaknesses. If the leader or manager is aware of the recurring shortcomings of individuals or joint skills, remedial training is planned and conducted to improve these specific performance areas.

The individual example sends an important message to the whole team: improving the organization is everyone's responsibility. The team's efforts to address its shortcomings are more powerful than any other lecture. (Reimer, 2006).

2.3 Leadership theory:

- Trait theory
- Behavior theory
- Contingency theory
- Situational theory

2.3.1 Trait theory:

The structure of the Trait comes from the view of behaviors that identify or explore that key traits of successful leaders.

It was believed that this theory could be summed up in key leadership traits that could be isolated and that people with such traits could then apply for a job, be selected, be prepared and trained to do or be harassed Leadership positions. This concept was popular in the military and is still used as a criterion for selecting candidates to select leadership positions.

Proponents of the theory say that leaders are born with the characteristics needed to distinguish themselves from those who are close to them or who are competing with them. They see leaders as heroes who have achieved great things in resolving disputes between themselves and their supporters.

This theory has been dubbed the Great Man's Thought, and has been wellreceived by the historians as the "Great Man Vision" as in the past the role of men only in leadership, and has been denied or overlooked in the role of women in leadership. This idea was unnecessary after much research and studies conducted on leadership and indicated that both men and women could have leader's skills. (Maj Earl Russel, 2011)

If men's leadership is natural born, can women themselves be born to be good leaders? Examples they used this believe this theory are including: Mao Zedong, Abraham Lincoln, Mahatma Gandhi, Alexander the Great, Adolf Hitler, etc., are one of the most famous leaders in the history of mankind. Both ancient and present history of world is considered those leaders to have a natural talent and an extraordinary personality that has helped them to excel in leadership.

One of the key problems with the Great Man's vision of leadership is that all people with so-called natural leadership traits actually become serious and world-famous leaders. If leadership is easily recognized as a birthright and a unique personal trait, then all people with the necessary traits will eventually see themselves as having a leadership role and have the right to dominate, others to be their own followers.

There is usually no or very few leaders with the desired characteristics when it comes to examining the characteristics of a leader (Zaccaro, 2007). In recent times, a variety of research findings have yielded extensive reviews of the concept of historically studied leadership characteristics (Derue et al., 2011; Hoffman et al., 2011; Judge et al. , 2009; Zaccaro, 2007). There are different ways to identify a leader; therefore, the last two allocations were organized by (1) social statistics and performance as interpersonal communication and interpersonal skills and (2) distal (characteristic) vs. proximal.

Based on a recent review of the results of research related to leadership, Derue et al. people, work knowledge, and social characteristics. In the census, gender has so far received the most attention in terms of leadership. Most scholars who comment on this issue understand that leaders from both sexes are equally effective and can have good leadership qualities.

This is assessed by the ability of the task to relate to how well individuals perform, complete and perform their tasks and how successful they are (Bass & Bass, 2008). In conclusion, the specific personal characteristics required of a leader relate to how a leader deals with social interaction.

Hoffman divided the issue into different categories, intelligence grouping, Morality, Experience Openness, and Sensitivity in this section. In conclusion, the specific personal characteristics required of a leader relate to how a leader deals with social interactions finally, personal characteristics relate to how a leader deals with social interactions. According to Hoffman and others (2011).

2.3.2   Behavior theory:

Behavioral leadership theory is based on a management perspective that values leaders based on the actions and behaviors they display in the workplace. People who support this theory believe that all you need to do to be an effective leader is to learn specific leadership qualities. If you want to be an effective leader or introduce a new leadership style, you can benefit from learning the theory of behavioral leadership.

This theory based on behavioral leadership argues that the success of a leader depends on their behavior rather than natural traits. The theory of moral leadership observes and evaluates the leader's actions and attitudes in response to a particular situation.

Proponents of her case have been working to make the actual transcript of this statement available online. People who believe in this theory believe that anyone can be a successful leader if they are able to learn and implement certain characteristics of a leader. The concept of moral leadership is very good in several areas.

This theory supports the notion that all leaders are capable of learning and developing leadership qualities through useful behaviors that are practiced in their workplaces. The vision of ethical leadership also encourages leaders to be aware of their culture and to recognize how it affects the productivity and morale of the employees they lead.

It is assumed leadership is based on the belief that great leaders are made, not born to be a leaders.
• People who believe this behavior in relation to this leadership theory focuses on the actions of leaders and not on the mental qualities or characteristics within the leader's personality.
• From this perspective, people can learn to be leaders through education and experience.
• Those believe Behaviorism theory thinking that anyone who adopts the right attitude can be a good leader.

Benefits of Behavioral Theory - It is naturally a pleasing theory. It serves as a benchmark against personal leadership characteristics and can be evaluated. This theory Provides detailed knowledge and understanding of the characteristics of a leader in the leadership selection process.

Limitation of Fraud View. There will be some personal judgment to determine who is deemed to be 'good' or 'winner' leader. There is also controversy over the most important characteristics of an effective leader. Different people have different views on this issue.

2.3.3 Contingency theory

The immediate view of leadership assumes that the effectiveness of a leader depends on whether their leadership style is appropriate for a particular situation or not. According to this theory, an individual can be an effective leader in one situation and an ineffective leader in another situation. Then no leader can succeed at all times and in any particular task assigned to him or her: when he or she is sent to another situation or when things around him or her may change they may not be able to achieve the expected success.

They include: Fiedler's Contingency Theory, the Situational Leadership Theory, the Path-Goal Theory and the Decision-Making Theory.

Connectivity VROOM-JAGO MODELFIEDLER'S Model Fiedler estimates that team performance depends on: The leadership style, described in terms of work motivation and relationship motivation.
• Preference for the situation, summarized in three ways: Member-Leader Relationship - The title of leader accepted and supported by team members. Position power is the ability of a leader to control his subordinates through reward and punishment.

Blanchard situation theory- Hersey-Blanchard Crisis Leadership Theory was created by Dr Paul Hersey and Ken Blanchard. The theory states that instead of using only one method, successful leaders should change their leadership styles based on the maturity of the people they lead and the details of the task. With this vision in mind, leaders should be able to focus more or less on the task.

2.3.4 The importance of leadership and personal development

The importance of leadership and personal development needs of organizations in the production, there is a wide understanding of the marketing departments of companies want employees who are new to the job or those whom are in the recruiting process. Experts in tourism and hospitality have proven that the individual has a very high burden during the recruitment process, although of course, when new job seekers are hired, it is necessary to have this wonderful personality of happiness and the rapture with the attraction at all times.

The leadership abilities of a particular job seeker are also examined in the way they present or prepare for job interviews and by considering the way they have managed and their work experience. Businesses are doing generally for profit purpose and do not want to lose millions of dollars, or lost their loyal customers.

Incidents such as blinding customers or treating them badly and annoying customers and not getting the trust and respect they deserve from the company, this can lead to customers being unhappy with the way they are being treated and not returning to the site. They can deal with other companies where they can meet their needs.

It is important that each leader spends a lot of time developing his or her personality and being happy with it to be succeeded in everything what he does. It is important to understand his personality and his friends or others who will help him understand the difference between words of success and failure and how to deal with them. It can be developed in general as well as his own personal character.

It can help him gain a better outlook, improve his culture, learn good relationships, build confidence, and develop a healthy body. It will also help him feel more confident in meeting other people in the business community and providing a variety of other services.

When it comes to leadership, personal development would go a long way in empowering your guests by passing on what the person already has. This includes his physical characteristics, his knowledge, his skills that align with his vision and positive values.

Strategies can be viewed in different ways, based on what has been achieved in the past and may not be achieved in the future, because the world is changing society and technology and people's interests are changing. The context and situation need to change, at least, to be re-evaluated, reviewed and updated.

If not available now, there is no strategic vision to follow for your company and the pace of progress will be slow and can lead to delays and lack of progress. Defining a strategic vision is the starting point as issues related to business management and management are always ongoing.

Personal development will also be supportive and helpful to ensure that the leader will be able to expand the needs and interests of his or her employees and clients. People who work with some of the leaders of big organizations and experts in business management explained that companies need the right people with the following characteristics to meet the demands.

1. Improve strengths and develop weaknesses
2. Use the right symbols and visuals needed for a good leader.
3. Control your emotions and feelings especially in difficult situations.
4. Building a better expression of views on leadership and personality to the world company

A leader must have the ability or skills to achieve the goals and objectives of the people he or she manages and to produce effective results. Behavior and personality willingness are equally important. When we say happy personality, it is the person who can create goodwill and respect that can lead to the desired success.

To achieve this requires extra effort, maturity, talent, and the ability to create good ideas and the capability to interact with different people in different situations. Literally it does not mean that a person has visual cues but is a person with acknowledgeable acceptance as expressed in the way he or she interacts with other people or expresses him self or herself to other co-workers or customers.

2.4 Leadership styles:

The author discussed above the leadership theory and we focused the following section the leadership style. The leadership style has the following componenets:

1. Autocratic (Authoritarian)
2. Bureaucratic
3. Democratic
4. Laissez-Faire
5. Coercive
6. Transactional
7. Transformational

2.4.1 Autocratic:

The Authoritarian leadership style is exemplified when the leader orders policies and procedures, decides the goals to be achieved, and directs and controls all activities without subordinate meaningful participation. Such a leader takes full control of the group, leaving the local self-government within the group.

The leader has a vision goal and should be able to effectively motivate their team to complete the task. The team is expected to complete the tasks under close supervision, while the unlimited power belongs to the leader. The answers below for orders given will be penalized or rewarded.

(Cherry,2012) Authoritarian leader are commonly called "autocrat". In some cases, they provide a clear idea of what needs to be done, when it should be done, and how it should be done.

There is often a clear conflict between the leader and the people under his control.) Altemeyer(1998) has conducted extensive research on what he calls the power of right wing Authoritarianism(RWA), and presented analysis on the types of personality of authoritarian leaders and those whom support him

Dictatorship leaders make decisions independently and with little or no consultation with the team they work with at all. Their supporters assists strict control by directly setting rules, procedures, and actions alone.

Dictatorships build great distances between themselves and their followers with the aim of bridging the gap between leadership and the people it governs. Hackman, et Jonson (2009). This type of leadership originated with the first tribes and kingdoms in the world. It is often used today when there is a small error occurs, such as construction work or other production work.

Leadership-Toolbox. (2008) Leading a dictatorship typically fosters less creative decision-making. Lewin also found it harder to move from a dictatorship to a more democratic one. Abuse of this style is often seen as authoritarian, authoritarian and dictatorial. Dictatorship can best be applied in the current situation where there is little time for group discussions to debate the issue.

2.4.2 Bureaucratic leaders

Bureaucratic is called "is the book manager" what he believes is ¨

•Everything must be done in a process or policy - When considering leadership traits, Integrity is often listed as one of the most valuable traits a leader can have.
 • If the book manager is not covered, the manager will refer to the next step above him or her.
 • This practice is practiced by officials including the Police and Military Officer.
 When to use Bureaucratic leadership
 • Carrying out daily activities
 • When required by standard and procedures
 • Using hazardous or fragile materials
 • Conducting security-related training
 • Activities that require seizing or receiving a cash.

 When not using the employment office. This method is not effective when:
 • When employees lose interest in their work and that of their co-workers.
 • Employees perform only what is expected of them and will not do any more work
 Who are the Bureaucratic Leaders? Law enforcement absolutely requires leaders at all times and free exchange, or needs to manage the money, we hope to have Bureaucratic leaders, people with Bureaucratic skills in their positions.

2.4.3 Participatory (Democratic) Leadership

Lewin's study found that participatory decision making, known as democratic leadership, is usually the most effective form of leadership. Democratic leaders not only guide team members well, but also engage the team and allow team members to make suggestions and participate in important recommendations and issues related to decision-making how to do the job. In Lewin's study, the children in this group were less productive than the members of the control group, but their productivity was higher than the others.

Participant leaders encourage team members to participate in decision-making process and decision-implementation, but they have the final say in the group's decision making process. Team members feel engaged and motivated and creative. Democratic leaders seem to make their followers feel like they are an important part of the team, which helps and encourages the team to achieve its goals and accomplish the work we want to do.

Often referred to as participatory mode

- Informs staff facilitates group discussion, often referred to as participatory leadership style
- Help staff evaluate their performance
- Allows staff to set goals
- Encourages employees to grow and be promoted

When to use Democracy
- Inform staff about what is happening
- Encourage staff to be involved in decision-making and problem-solving in the team.
- Provide opportunities for employees to develop a high sense of personal growth and job satisfaction
- Solve complex problems that need more planning.
- Encourage team building and participation.

When Democracy Is Not Used
- Democratic leadership should not be used when:
- When there is not enough time to get everyone's advice.
- It is easier and cheaper for the manager to make the decision.
- The organization or company cannot afford to make mistakes related to the execution of the work.
- The manager feels threatened by this type of leadership.
There may also be serious concerns about worker safety

2.4.4 Deligative leadership (Laissez-Faire)

Lewin found that children working in delegation leadership, also known as laissez-faire leadership, were the most productive of all the other groups compared. The children of this group also sent more demands to the leader, showed together little work, and unable to work independently.

Delegate leaders give little or no guidance to team members and leave it to team members to make decisions. While this approach can be useful in situations involving highly qualified professionals, it often leads to poor, undefined roles and lack of motivation.

Lewin noted that the laissez-faire leadership tends to result in groups that have no direction and members blame each other for mistakes, refuse to accept personal responsibility, make little progress, and produce little work.

Laissez-faire's leadership is characterized by the following:
• A hands-on approach that allows employees to lead and do the work
• Leaders provide all training and support.
• Decisions are left to the staff
• Mistakes are tolerated but corrected
• Accountability falls on the leader

Although the common term for this style is "laissez-faire" which means complete handshake, many leaders are still open and available to team members for consultation and feedback. Leaders may provide direction for the start of the project, but then allow team members to carry out their work under very limited supervision.

This leadership style is demanding greater trust between the leader and his subordinates. The leaders should feel confident that the team members have the skills, knowledge, experience to carried out the duties, and sits to follow to complete the project without micromanage's been made.

Like other forms of leadership, the laissez-faire leadership style has its advantages.

• Promotes personal growth. Because leaders are open-minded in their own style, employees have the opportunity to take responsibility and perform the work themselves. This leadership style creates an environment conducive to the growth and development of employees.
• Encourages creativity and creates something new or classifies a new way of doing work. The freedom given to employees can encourage creativity and the thought of developing something new to add to the work.
• Allows quick decision-making. In the absence of micromanagement, employees under the leadership of laissez-faire have self-management to make their decisions and carry out the expected work. They are able to make quick decisions without having to wait long for the work permit approval process.

Some possible disadvantages of this method of laissez-faire include:

• Role instability: In some cases, the laissez-faire style leads to undefined roles within the group. Since team members receive little leadership or feedback, they may not really be sure of their role in the team work and what they are supposed to be doing in their time.

• Low leader involvement in the work team: Laissez-faire leaders are often seen as unconnected and have no influence on what is going on, which can lead to a lack of coordination within the group. As the leader seems to be indifferent to what is happening, his

followers sometimes raise this issue and show no concern for the implementation of this project.
• Low accountability: Some leaders take advantage of this approach to avoid taking responsibility for team failures as a result of the work being done. When goals are not achieved, the leader may then accuse team members of not completing tasks or failing to perform the tasks expected of them.
• Passivity: Worst of all, laissez-faire leadership stands for laziness or even avoiding real leadership. In such cases, these leaders do nothing, try to motivate their followers, cannot recognize the efforts of team members, and will not try to involve the group.

2.5 Leadership style theory

The issue of leadership is so broad that it can be viewed from different angles, and scholars have differing views. Some say leadership is not learned, it is born, while others say it is not born but can be achieved through education, experience and capability.

I think it is not a matter of being born a leader, it is a matter of learning when one acquires the skills one needs and I think a leader should have a combination of two people who are born with a strong leadership and also have a strong personality, good ability to lead people. In addition to personality and ability, there is a need for knowledge of leadership and experience in the work to be done.

I agree with the idea based on the belief that great leaders are made, not born to be leaders. This view is supported by the behavior theory of the skinner and its host as mentioned above.

The other Trait theory, which we have mentioned above, believes that the leader is born of Charisme, which is why they use the word Great man to mean that the leader is born and cannot be reborn.
The difference between a known and an unknown leader is to recognize the characteristics of a good leader, such as: the leader knows that you have the right ability, courage, and drive to take action to achieve your goals.

Trait theory holds that 1/3 of the skills a leader possesses are born, while 2/3 of those skills are believed to be acquired by a leader through education and experience and personal development.

Cole (2004) Another important point is that it is difficult for a charisma-born leader not to have strong personalities or traits in order to gain influence over those under his leadership.

Mr. Cole (2004 states that a leader needs to have:
- Skills
- Principles

- Knowledge
- Personality

I would add that it is also necessary for the leader to have the ability to perform an important task. It is also important that the process of leadership depends on the leader, the task being performed and the purpose and situation of the environment in which the task is to be performed.

This relates to the skills, needs and motivations of the people he or she works with. It can also be influenced by the goals of the people you work with, personal relationships and surroundings. In the context of the environment in which the work is to be done, it is important to have a close relationship with the team, cultural issues, external pressures and available resources.

Indeed (September, 2020) Leadership identifies unique leader personality that differentiates recognized leaders and non-leaders. They are founded on the vision that leaders are 'born, not made' (that is, that leadership is often born, rather than created).

When attempting to be a good leader, it is predominant to recognize and ehance the basic values of your leadership. Perceiving what leadership values are and what the basics of leadership values you want to take in your leadership style can help you improve your relationships and closeness with your team, and thus become an influence leader.

2.5. 1 What is the value of leadership?

The value of leadership is the key issues and principles that guide our personal and professional lives. Your values can be defined as the factors that you consider to be most important in achieving your goals and being happy. Leadership values are closely linked to both your individual core values and your company values.

Why are leadership values important?

Leadership values are important because they assist you in deciding how you want to achieve your goals and what kind of leader you want to be. Your core values of leadership contribute to how you make decisions and the steps you take each day. This allows you to influence issues with your team in a positive way that encourages high performance and excellence.

Here is a list of basic leadership values:
• Impact
• Vision
• Honesty
• Enthusiasm
• Honesty

- Decision making
- Compassion
- Personal development
- Service
- Respect
- Resilience
- Adaptation
- Confirmation

2.6 Business management and leadership Pros and cons

McBain(2019) conducted a research for advantages and disadvantages of good or bad leadership and explored that the biggest disadvantage is the level of complexity you face. Let's start with the benefits.

Most leaders want to have more responsibilities than they already have, and they want the responsibility to shape existing work, as well as come up with new ideas in order to achieve this, you need more resources, power and people under your control. And there are far more to it than that in terms of status, money to strengthen position in their power.

When you are a leader you have a greater chance of finding the complexity of the work and designing it in a positive way, and you can shape that. On the other hand, the negative side you can be overwhelming of the job.

Here I am specifically talking about leading people. Of course it is wonderful to work with people, to have encouraging discussions, to see how several minds work on a problem that they can achieve together. Together we rejoice in the achievement.

Complexity can lead to mental fatigue and can be overwhelming for a leader, especially for others' complexity, emotional devices, demands, feelings and personal motivations. All these demands are put on you by all sides, and while still trying to achieve the goal you set, it is a tricky mind. It will put a strain on every human being. But there is still no way to prepare people for this better. Bray (2018) explored what are the pros and cons of being a leader?

2.6. 1 Pros

1. As a leader you can gain insight and create a culture in which thinking is practiced. When you are just a regular employee doing various jobs, you used to see my superiors as incompetent and misguided, which made me frustrated. Now, as a leader, you make sure that you do your best to create a complete positive message and vision that can be implemented by making the executive decision independent and empowered. People want to be a part of and manage something bigger or beyond them selves which can be a success.

2. The leader receives energy and enthusiasm that motivates you to do something. What makes a leader happy is that he or she enjoys a feeling of joy and happiness. When you show your emotions and show enthusiasm in those around you are working with because you can share the emotions can be infectious. It's hard for other people with the feeling that the noise of the positive energy.

3. If you lead your subordinates correctly you can be seen as right. I focus and enjoy the confidence in myself that I feel is well connected to my team below me. Don't be fooled and try not to think about what is "good" for what you think the leader is behaving like not true.

2.6.2 Cons

You should take responsibility for leading the team, and the results, good or bad, will come back to haunt you and you should be able to deal with these work related challenges and improve the performance of your entire team which is the way to success.

You should be able to cope with the huge amount of stress that can come from different sources, which can confuse you. Consumers, personnel issues, service issues or products that are able to perform a variety of tasks to keep the work going and also achieve the desired goal.

You are expected to enjoy being a "leader song". You are central to the good and the bad. You lead the team and you have the greatest influence on the success or failure of your tasks that reflect your goals.

2.7 Suggestions how to improve business leadhership?

Business Leadership is a long journey that aims to achieve success, stimulating and motivating the team you lead is essential to achieving the specific goals of the organization or company. Finding a way to motivate yourself and build your team spirit is the key to moving forward and succeeding.

Good Leadership & Competence play an important role in driving the success of an organization or company that moves it forward. Leaders guide the company to the goals they want to achieve, and help them achieve those goals. Leaders are dynamic, passionate and inspiring. Leadership into the possibility of the realization of the truth and or to achieve the vision of the Association.

Take note of these guidelines to strengthen self-motivation, motivate others and develop your leadership skills:

1.   Inspire yourself

The real motivation is within your self. Find what motivates you, and see your goals. Without motivation, we would not be able to lead our team.

Motivation provides the desire to do what is necessary to achieve a goal. Motivation comes from within, but it is influenced by the actions and words of others. The role of the leader in motivation is to understand the needs and wants of others, to adapt and promote the driving individuals of the team's goals, and to influence others to achieve those great goals.

2. Think about the others

Be careful with people, tell them you trust them and want the best for your team. Leaders are examples of people below them, good and bad in the workplace, every action they take or every statement they make while at work or absent from work. Leaders must give a clear purpose to their supporters or subordinates and perform it in different ways. Leaders can use direct communication to achieve their goals through requests or instructions on what to do.

3. Encourage less enthusiastic staff

The best leaders should be able to redirect negativity in to motivation or positive thinking. Learn how to motivate your less- than-enthusiastic staff and you can grow your business to be the best it can be.

Do not be quick to dismiss or fire people who are lazy or showed negative behavior habits, try to motivate them and train them to build their skills and do the job well. .

This leadership style is demanding greater trust between the leader and his subordinates. The leaders should feel confident that the team members have the skills, knowledge experience to carried out the duties.

4.Recruit talented staff

In the same way you should avoid unhealthy relationships, and by encouraging employees to get lazy to do their job, make sure you open the door to those who provide motivation and satisfaction to the team with the skills and work experience.

5. Appeal of values

Find out what is important to your team and turn it into a driving force of motivation. Team values are important because they assist you in deciding how you want to achieve your goals and what kind of leader you want to be.

Your core values of leadership contribute to how you make decisions and the steps you take each day. This allows you to influence issues with your team in a positive way that encourages high performance and excellence.

6. Celebrate small achievements

No matter how small the success you and your team have had; it will be a great source of encouragement. Celebration success motivates employees and the workplace. It guides the staff to work better and leads the organization to more productivity and success.

7. Reward your team

There are many ways to reward good performance and the ability to achieve key goals. The team will see it as an encouragement to stay on the right track.

8. Trust and representation

Trust your team and delegate tasks. You will find that things can be done in many different ways and you will encourage creativity and new ideas.

9. Get involved with your team

Ask how they are helping each other. Encourage them to improve.

10. Be transparent

Share information with your team should be aware of the circumstances that affect the project or work for which they are involved.

11. Report problems

For this reason, you must report problems. Working together, the situation will be addressed more effectively and solutions and other solutions will be easier.

12. Congratulations don't point your finger

Avoid pointing fingers at a specific person when there are mistakes, on the contrary, try to focus on good performance whenever it happens. Positive feedback is fundamental to maintaining motivation and strengthening leadership.

13. Develop your team's potential

Start training your team to develop their skills, for example, time management. More than 500 companies, most of them international companies, have already implemented Triskelion, a production video course for their employees.

14. Need

Good leadership demands avoid neutrality. Real motivation only seems to go beyond overcoming problems.

15. Ask

Ask people what motivates them as well as what discourages them. Work to remove the depression equation and focus on promoting it.

16. Show "motivators"

Those who work enthusiastically and pass it on to the rest of the team. Make professional development a priority for these people.

17. Do not be afraid

Mistakes make you learn. Do not be afraid of possible mistakes because of the wrong decision making.

18. Finish what you started

Like Triskelion's video-game course in production and time management, do one thing at a time, and do it until the end. Avoid over eating to be more effective and aware of your progress.

19. Wrap up

Strengthen team unity by engaging in activities that change daily activities, for example, cultural activities, group buildings, or office meetings.

20. Don't give up!

The key to success is perseverance. Every leader knows that the notice is not optional, although it is wise to note how intellectual out.

What about you What do you do to be a good leader?

I don't think leadership is born for leadership, and leadership is something to be learned. The leader must then have leadership competencies so that he or she can lead the team better.

The most important thing is that the leader has good relation and communication skills and can explain his or her thoughts and ideas in writing and orally so that the task can be carried out effectively.

As a leader, it is important:
1. to have the attention of the person you want to communicate with by creating and maintaining eye contact.
 2) Try to send the same clear messages in terms of speech size. To get it, make sure the volume and volume you are using matches the content of the message you sent. As the old proverb: "Actions speak louder than words." Means taking action is better to speack allot.

Personal Development is essential for a leader to grow and gain more knowledge and experience to be a successful leader. The Big Five theory refers to the 5 behaviors reported and marked as follows:

• Transformation - tends to be open, active and social
• Openness - tends to enjoy diversity, innovation, competition and academics
• Nervous Stimulus - prone to experiencing negative emotions
• Acceptance - towards friendship, kindness and cooperation
• Awareness of self-discipline and self-control
• Each of these five factors is really a kind of two opposing partners: segregation and prevention, openness and closeness, nervousness and emotional stability, coping and hostility, conscience and conflict.
• Appreciate art, emotion, interest, extraordinary ideas, interest, and diverse experiences.
• a tendency to organize and rely on self dependence, self discipline, objective, and planning preferences rather than unpredictable behavior.

A good leader must: (1) motivate and energize (2) gather information (3) make decisions and (4) organize our lives.
1. Persuasion: Persuasion means changing one's mind. If the mind is not changed, the person is not satisfied.
2. Delegation: One of the most common methods of overcoming limitation to learn how to assign work to others. If you do this well, you can quickly build a strong and successful team and you will be able to meet the expectation of others.

2.8 Conclusion:

Possessing a good personal skills are a very important factors when it comes to leadership. As mentioned above there are different perspectives on good leadership, and the long road to achieve success, is one that needs to be looked at from many angles.

I believe that some people are born with good leadership qualities, but even if a person has strong personalities and the qualities required of a good leader yet, if he does not add to his knowledge and build his leadership personality we can say that something is lacking, which could have impact of the leadership qualities.

In my opinion a good leader is a person with good manners and strong personality who can make decisions and lead a team.

Suppose you are given a new car key and you were told to own it, however you never drive a car. No matter how clever you are, you can't drive that car, and if you try to drive it without proper training and driving license. You will make a big mistakes and you at risk to committed an accident and taking a risk for yourself and others.

Then no matter how good you are you need to learn and adapt how the car being driven and things to be lead. That means you are not only required to get practice how to drive a car, but you need to have theory how to drive a car.

I then support the fact that leadership is not born and can be learned according through education, training, practice and couching. I supported to the Behaviorism Theory?

I also believe that there is no leader who is good and could lead in every situation and everything. Every leader has unique traits which suitable to lead in some situations that is good according to situational theory.

I also think that there is a need to constantly develop and build the qualities required of a good leader and that the leader should always undertake knowledge, continuous personal development throughout one's life because education is a life long process.

There are also leadership styles and the most popular are Autocrat, democratic and Laissez-Faire . In each case, they have seized it, despite obstacles we can scarcely imagine. " For example Autocrat can be used when the team does not have enough time to discuss for the work or task, which is expected to be performed.

It is bad for a leader to always make important decisions about the job and the team he is working with. In this scenario mostly employees perform the job because they have no other choice. They are aware if they don't do it they are risked to lose their jobs.

The advantage of democratic leadership's that decisions related the work are shared and consulted, as well as decisions that come from top up and bottom down, and this is due to the team's cooperation and the relationship between the team and their leader who is always good and is being loved in the team, and the staff.

Employees feel that they belong to the association and that they are related with the company. The employees feel that they are being respected and their rights and interest are protected. The problem is that everything is debated for a long time and no quick decision can be made to carry out the task quickly.

Laissez-Faire leadership is best done by professional people who do not require strong leadership, who do the work on an individual or team basis without any instructions from the leader. The leader's job is only to sign letters, and the work is done by the team with minimum or less supervision from the team leader. The problem is not being able to make the right decisions at the right time, and being a team that works individually and not as a team and that leads to negative work.

It is also clear that the leader is not always taking responsibilities, if anything goes wrong he will be held accountable, but the leader accountability is not the responsibility of the team, if the things are not doing correctly, the blame directed the staff and not leader him self.

2.9 Recommendations:

So while I personally consider democratic leadership to be the best leadership styles, there are advantages and disadvantages to each. Depending on the situation and the type of work to be done and the timing, it is planned to carry out the task at hand and it cannot be said that this type of leadership is the best and is appropriate for the current situational leadership style.

Great leaders don't just tell you what to do, however they show you how to conduct the job or task you are expected to perform. As an old proverb said" Actions speak louder than words"

When the organization provides leaders/managers with the necessary leadership training it will also increase staff leadership & and the best performance of duties, which can be achieved in the areas of education & development.

The leader of a group or army is important, because the success and failure of the group depends on the person leading and the style of the leadership. Any leader with good decision-making, creativity, self-confidence and possessed extreme motivation encourage is closer to success than a leader without these traits.

As Alexander the Great stated a herd of sheep led by a lion is better than a group of lions led by a sheep. As the lion is stronger not only physically, but psychologically, and emotionally, he can better attacking targeting the enemy and better defense himself and his team.

"An army of sheep led by a lion is better than an army of lions led by a sheep." Alexander the Great.

.

To be a leader you have to take responsibility so that you become important and trustworthy, and at the same time respectable. Have you ever heard the phrase: "To lead, you must first being lead someone else" - Laozi

It means setting an example for commanding and respecting the leader. Every day you should strive to be present and witness everything you see to have a worthy goal. That means every aspect of your life, from your family to your social friends to your dreams.

Reliance however does not depend on the rules; it is to understand how necessary it is in any circumstance to create rules. Being a leader at first is a daunting task, many seem to say "think outside the box" but that is lazy and meaningless advice. Those who understand this phrase never need it and those who do not get it heard.

2.10 References:

1. Altemeye, B(1998) The Other "Authoritarian Personality" by Bob r Advances in Experimental Social PsychologyVolume 30, 1998, Pages 47-92

2. Bass, B. M. & Bass, R. (2008). *The Bass handbook of leadership: Theory, research, and managerial applications* (4th ed.). New York: Free Press.

3. Bray, E. (2018). What ar the pros-and con-of being aleader. *https://www.quora.com, retreived on 27 November 2020*

4. Cherry, K(2020). "Lewin's Leadership Styles." About.com Psychology. Web. 18 November. 2020. <http://psychology.about.com/od/leadership/a/leadstyles.htm>.

5. Derue, D. S., Nahrgang, J. D., Wellman, N., & Humphrey, S. E. (2011). Trait and behavioral theories - of leadership: An integration and :meta-analytic test of their relative validity. *Personnel Psychology, 4(1),* 7-52.

6. Indeed(2020) Leadership values/www.indeed.com/career-advice/career-development/leadership-values.Retrieved 12-11-2020

7. Hackman, M. Z., & Johnson, C. E. (2009). Leadership: A Communication Perspective (5th ed.). Long Grove, IL, Waveland Press.

8. Hoffman, B. J., Woehr, D. J., Maldagen-Youngjohn, R., & Lyons, B. D. (2011). Great man or greatvmyth? A quantitative review of the :relationship between individual differences and leader effectiveness. *Journal of Occupational and Organizational Psychology, 84(2),* 347-381.

9. Marshall, G. (2016). Leaders Make Values Visible. *https://www.designtoolbox.co.uk/strategies/leaders-make-values-visible/* .

10. McBain, L. (2019). What are the advantanges and disadvantages of a leader. *https://www.quora.com* .

11. Nodeson, S. B. (2012). Interdisciplinary Journal of Contemporary Research in Business. *tps://www.researchgate.net/publication/282639942_INTERDISCIPLINARY_JOURNAL_OF _CO* , Volg 4, No

12. Russel, M. E. (2011). Leadership Theories andStyle: A Transitional Approach.Military Leadership Writing Competition,CGSC Class 11-02. *Writing Competition,CGSC Class 11-02.*

13. *Kirkpatrick, Shelley A.; <u>Locke, Edwin A.</u> (1991). <u>"Leadership: Do traits matter?"</u> (PDF). Academy of Management Executive. **5** (2). Archived from <u>the original</u> (PDF) on 2010-06-27.*

14. Kirkpatrick, S. A., & Locke, E. A. (1991). Leadership: Do traits matter? Archived from the original (PDF) on 2010-06-27. *Academy of Management Executive. 5 (2). , 5 (2).*

15. Leadership-Toolbox. (2008). Leadership Styles: Authoritarian Leadership. Retrieved November 15, 2013, from <u>http://www.leadership-toolbox.com/autocratic-leadership.html</u>

16. Lewin K, L. R. (1939). Patterns of aggressive behavior in experimentally created "social climates". J Soc Psychol. 1939;10(2):271-301. *J Soc Psychol* , 271-301.

17. Marshall, G. (2016). Leaders Make Values Visible. *https://www.designtoolbox.co.uk/strategies/leaders-make-values-visible/* retreived 27 Novem.2020

18. McBain, L. (2019). What are the advantanges and disadvantages of a leader. *https://www.quora.com,*retrieved 27 November 2020.

19. Russel, M. E. (2011). Leadership Theories andStyle: A Transitional Approach.Military Leadership Writing Competition,CGSC Class 11-02.

20. Willink, J. a. (2017). *Extreme Ownership: How U.S. Navy SEALs Lead and Win.* New Yor: St. Martin's Pres.

21. Zaccaro, S. J. (2001). The nature of executive leadership: A conceptual and empirical analysis of success. Washington, DC, US: American Psychological Association.

22. Zaccaro, S. J. (2007). Trait-based perspectives of leadership. *American Psychologist, 62(1)*, 6-16.

23. Zaccaro, S. J., Kemp, C., & Bader, P. (2004). Leader traits and attributes. *The nature of leadership.* (pp. 101–124). Thousand Oaks, CA, US: :Sage Publications, Inc.

Chapter Three

3.Marketing Management:

Marketing management is the organizational behavior of a company in which organizations or companies study how best to get their business to market and how best to conduct marketing orientation, most relevant messages and media resources to find out and monitor and respond to market customers' responses.

Marketing management also helps the company operate the financial resources and create a competitive strategy to discuss the formal business model of the company.

These include Porter's 5 business forces.

Porter's 5 forces is an important marketing commentary that focuses on supporting entrepreneurs and business managers to monitor and account for the "market power balance" between various local and international companies, to comment, out of the attractiveness and potential benefits of the business sector. Here are the five armies:

• Competitive competition
• Replacement threats
• Buyer's bargaining power
• Threats to new arrivals
• Ability to negotiate with suppliers

Analysis of competitors, marketers creates visuals with reports that business competitors release to the market and then demonstrate their competitive strengths and weaknesses using a measurement system called SWOT analysis.

Marketing managers study the pricing strategy of each competitor, profit sources, resources and capabilities, competitive placement and product diversity, level of direct interaction, historical responses to industry development, and more.

Marketing managers often conduct market research to conduct marketing analysis. Marketers use a variety of techniques to conduct market research, but some of the most popular are:
• Qualitative market research, such as focus groups and different types of interviews
• Numerous market research, such as statistical survey
• Testing techniques such as test markets
• Observation techniques such as observation (location)

Marketing managers can design and monitor various local scans and competitive secret systems to help identify trends and inform the company's marketing analysis.

3.1 Customer Target Marketing Strategies

Sometimes a marketing strategy focuses on a specific customer who sends them messages or ads to arouse and attract their attention.

Another strategy that influences the marketing of a business is the competition of the stock market, which deals with popular brands and the use of price strategies to then attract the attention of customers who are interested in that particular business. Take, for example, Microsoft and Apple. Microsoft handles data, texting, soft data and emails making it the most productive and commercially viable.

Apple is in control of the graphic design market, which has given Apple products a good market share. They also offer apple pie and softball schools to students, who want to buy and become customers in the future when the students growth up.

Marketing management is about financial resources and competitive strategies to comment on the business operations of a company.

In this world we live in, there are many changes taking place at different speeds, which you can see today and not the same as yesterday, and tomorrow will be like this tomorrow or the next day, God willing. The marketing needs to keep pace with the constant changes in the areas in which the company operates and the overall changes in the world.

Marketing focuses on marketing realities such as globalization, changing technology, and efforts to control the economy

Marketing is really about understanding and recognizing the needs of people and society and how to meet these needs which include different areas of individual and social needs such as food, shelter, clothing, transportation etc. There is also a need to create new and emerging needs, in order to increase productivity.

Entrepreneurs look to the market for lucrative business opportunities using existing marketing.

3.2 Scope of Marketing

(Kotlar, 2000) Marketing professionals are engaged in marketing for 10 different types of organizations:

Products, services, costs, customers, locations, homes, organizations, information and views.

Products: The production of body parts operates in most countries in the commercial activities of the marketers.

In most countries there are a wide range of services, including goods such as clothing, food, electrical appliances, building materials, educational materials and medical equipment.

Services include airlines, hotels, maintenance, doctors, and other professions such as accountants and lawyers, engineers etc.

Events: Marketers promote up-to-date markets such as the Olympics, trade shows, games and art shows

Experience. By organizing several services and products, one can create, stage,and market experiences.

Familiar people.

Celebrity marketing has become a huge business venture. Advertising by celebrities such as artists, famous actors, doctors and lawyers and other professionals makes marketing using their brand name and has become a big business.

4. Urban Areas:

Municipalities, counties and tourism companies compete to attract tourists from home or abroad. .

5 Marketplaces: The market places of economic experts in the fields of development, real estate companies, commercial banks, and local flora and fauna include economics development experts, real estate agents, commercial banks, local businesses

6. Marketing also includes information from schools and universities, publishing companies, books, comedy and social media.

3.3 Overview of marketing activities

The marketers of commercial companies are skilled at increasing the demand for conference products and related marketing. This has affected and limited perceptions of the activities of the marketing management team of the company such as production and logistics. This is a task that the marketers are responsible for.

This is important for the company not to fabricate the products that are not needed in the market, because the marketers manage and are responsible for the market demand and are aware of the market and the needs of the customers who buy products por services of the company.

Marketers also study the market and are aware of customer needs and demands for products that are currently in demand, hidden needs, and strong needs in the market, and products that can satisfy existing customers.

They are also aware of declining demand in the market, persistent needs, current and non-urgent emergencies, and more needs that can be brought to the market. .

The objectives of marketing companies are to study the level, time available in the areas and countries in which the company operates and the different needs in those areas.

3.4 Decisions made by Marketers

Marketing managers are involved in many decisions about their product marketing activities, which can be very different such as product characteristics and design, planning and designing new products, hiring marketing staff, finances to spend on advertising and customer engagement.

Marketing managers also make simple decisions about the information, the colors of the new products, and the questions that marketers can ask the market.

3.5 Marketing Strategies:

(Išoraitė, 20014) Companies and organizations develop long-term action plans using strategies to achieve success in customer competition.

Organizations and companies use the resources they have, we mean the finances, personnel, machinery and equipment and real estate owned by companies.

The company uses its resources to keep abreast of developments in the company's operating environment, to attract and persuade customers and to purchase services and products sold by the company.

Every company strives to have a better place in the business market, in which they want to find effective ways to make a difference in the local and international market.

So entrepreneurs who are engaged in the marketing their various products who want to be successful in long term marketing, need to organize and develop their marketing plan, and need to choose a clear strategy to operate.

Strategic selection requires a study of the market and the opportunities available and the needs of the customers. It is also important to choose a marketing strategy and it is also important to consult with all stakeholders of the company.

Marketing strategy is a philosophy related to the way an organization or company needs groups and individuals to gain recognition for valuing, offering, communicating and reaching out to others. Strategy guides the direction and scope of long term activities reaching corporate entities to be competitive and profitable.

3.6 Marketing Objectives:

In order to achieve the marketing objectives set by an organization or company it is important, it is necessary to plan and formulate a clear strategy with long term future goals as well as feasibility that can be achieved and measured later.

The strategy should include evaluating the company's strengths and weaknesses, in order to maintain further develop the strengths and develop a plan to reinforce and strengthen the weaknesses.

It is also important to include in the strategy the potential problems that the company could face, in order to be taking prevention measures and to develop a plan to address it. It is also important to identify the indicators that need to be evaluating the company's marketing efforts in order to achieve the expected results of achieving market competition goal.

3.6.1 What are the marketing objectives?

(Indeed, 2021 Marketing objectives are essential to the success of the business goals and objectives of the company. These objectives often consist of a number of small steps that the marketing department then focuses on and takes to enable the company to achieve its business goals and marketing managers can make use of the smart Guidelines for goal creation.

This will enable the creation to ensure that the marketing target set by the company is the best direction, and that it can guide the organization in determining the campaign and how best to reach the target customers and clarify the real purpose of the marketing team of the company, including the following.

Specific, the marketing goal should be specific to the company and unique to an effective plan that can bring the company Profit.

Measurement: There must be a specific system for measuring progress toward goals, and if you fail to measure your goals, you must re-evaluate your goals and make changes or develop a goal plan and replace the previous one.

Achievable: you should evaluate your goal and then critically review it with the marketing team or marketing management, which can be achieved within a certain period of time, which also needs to be realistic, availeble, and can be achieved.

Relevant: It is also important to note that marketing objectives are related to the company's existing goals and values that define what the company stands for and its business goals.

Time-based: The goal should be to have a set time to start and a time to finish to reach the goal, a set time can lead to people being guided which is also encouraging can be accounted for. That if you are not able to achieve the goals you will understand why it needs to be achieved and its priorities.

It is also important to understand that marketing objectives are not the same as marketing goals although they are sometimes used interchangeably use a time, how to measure it and how to describe it. Marketing goals are designed to last a long time and are paired with the company's overall goals and objectives.

3.7 Marketing management functions

(Sharma, 2015) made a presentation and highlighted the market management task and summarizing the following:

1. Marketing management activities are related to developing marketing strategies and identifying potential opportunities in the long run.
2. Study and measure the market and the areas and understand the customer's desire for profitable market opportunities and how best to develop the markets to be targeted.
3. Choosing and determining the wholesale and retail prices, price reductions, and loan repayment methods.
4. Set the right price for the business to be delivered to the target market.
5. Strengthen the linkages for the communication value sufficient for the targeting market.
6. Rapid price growth and growth of new products, testing and presentation as part of time view.

3.9 Development of Marketing Concept

3.9.1 Creating a marketing information system

We are talking about monitoring the inside and outside of the company, and it is important to note that there are four components to the marketing process, namely:
1. Internal marketing
2. Marketing intelligence system
3. Marketing research
4. Decision support system.

The creation of a marketing system can be strengthened by the following:

1 Building customers relationships

Marketing is necessary to strengthen the relationship between the company and the customers, building a customer relationship is a system that is vital and profitable for the business, and to sustain the transfer market and can be developed through the use of emerging concepts such as marketing communication maintain and work to strengthen the relationship between the customer and the company.

2. Making strong Brands

In order to profit from marketing it is necessary for the business to be branded strong and different from other businesses in the market. Private branding is one of the marketing activities, and the brand also helps in the development and growth of the business, expanding business marketing, product placement and business services.

3. Determining the integration mix

When conducting product marketing, it is necessary to create an effective marketing integration solution in order to meet the customer needs of the target markets. Marketers use a variety of marketing tools including pricing, business location and advertising issues, which in turn can greatly enhance marketing and meet different customer needs.

4. Paying the price

When it comes to marketing it is important to reach the target customers, the price of the product is important and the difference between the price of the customer to the product, and whether the product or service they bought is worth the price. The price should not be higher than the price of other similar products in the market in the first place, nor should it be significantly lower than the market value of that product or service in the market. Consumer choice of product or service is determined and guided by price which should always be taken into account.

7. The cost of communication

Marketing is also essential for a good and effective delivery of the market, which requires the use of an integrated marketing program to achieve the right target market. This requires that the company personally and collectively convey its message to its customers. It is important for the marketing department to establish a multi-faceted communication system such as advertising, personal sales, sales promotion, strengthening public relations and using different types of marketing.

8. Create long-term growth

Marketing should also have strategies and tactics related to its production and branding. It is also important to do something to increase productivity. It focuses on placement, development of new products, testing and launch of sales and use.

9. Implement and control

Marketing should plan its marketing products that it needs to control its marketing plans. In which case businesses need to build a well-organized marketing system, it is also important to keep track of what has been planned and what challenges they face or budget plans through a budget plan. And this could be accountable answer to existing marketing plans and business strategies.

3.10 Marketing values:

The power of marketing helps:

• Creating a demand for the products and services provided by the company, which is essential for the economic growth of the company.
• Enabling job creation
• Delivering company resources so that the company can contribute to the development and social services in the areas where the company operates.
• Build and maintain a good relationship with the customers and remain a loyalty, and respected the company.
• Marketers decide which guidelines, prices and markets to spend on advertising, selling and marketing costs on social media in areas where customers, competition and technology are safe.
• If marketers are not careful then they can fail in market competition. They should constantly improve their pricing and marketing strategies, in order to the satisfaction of their employees, company shareholders, logistics and distributors of goods and channels.
• Marketers support the company to adapt and grow in the changing environment in which the organization operates and the changes that are taking place.

Philip Kotler holds that:

Morgen, W (2003)."the organization's marketing task is to determine the needs, wants and interests of target markets and to achieve the desired results more effectively and efficiently than competitors, in a way that preserves or enhances the consumer's or society's well-being.

3.11 Understanding customer needs, wants and demands

(Cimorelli, T(2021) As mentioned above marketing is one of the most important business management activities performed business companies. So it is important to note that marketers do not create demand. But marketers want to know the needs of their customers in the market so that they can meet the needs of the market and sell their existing products or services.

Key concepts in marketing include understanding and meeting the needs, desires and demands of the targeted customers to be focused.

Needs are something that satisfies the basic needs of the customer or human being. Needs is the desire or demand for specific products or services that a person needs. Orders are specific products that the customer is willing or able to pay for or purchase.

Marketers must constantly research the needs of their customers in the market in order to make a profitable business and taking the benefit for the market competition.

It is important that the needs of the customers in the market are clear and understand the type of product, the characteristics of the products, their color, etc., as well as the reasonable price of the product to attract the customers, as well as the company benefits.

As mentioned earlier, companies or organizations should have a specific budget to implement effective marketing, and it is recommended that businesses create a specific budget so that they can be used for marketing expenses, some marketing experts estimated that company to spend the marketing activities not less than 10% of the company's budget.

No matter how much effort is put into the company's expenses, first and foremost marketing, it is still difficult for companies to win market competition if there are no specific costs to spend on marketing the company's ads to attract customers and provide market opportunities for the sale of goods or services.

It is important that all the products and services of the company are able to better meet the needs of the customers to gain the trust of the company and customer to remain loyal to the company or the organization.

And there are customers who are different, they always desiresto get the benefit of the product or business they bought so that they can satisfy their personal or group needs. This is not an easy task, and requires a system of sorting the product, a structure that suits different segments of the customer so that their needs are understood.

It is important for the entrepreneur to be aware of these issues and being flexible in using them at the lowest possible cost, and it is important to develop products new products with different characteristics and colors.

3.12 The five key product levels are:

(CGMA, 2021) highlighted Philip Kotler, a marketing strategist who recognizes that customers have five key needs:

1. Basic Benefits:

The basic needs or desires of the customers are satisfied by using the company's product or service. For example digital images.

2. General products:
Some products to have special characteristics in order to satisfy the customers. For example, DGT images can be customized by the general computer and can be used with standard graphics software.

3. Expected Products:

Characteristics or style that customers expect to have the product they are buying. For example, a computer is designed to filter out fast digital images.

4. Extended Products:
Add imported products with more useful features, unique features so that it is different from other products that compete with the market, for example a computer with the tools and software it operates at no extra cost or having additional discounts.

5. Possible products:

This product is accompanied by all the additions and structural changes that may be made to the product in the near future, since it looks at how loyal customers are to the company's business, which is expected to delight customers.

This is followed by changes in the characteristics of the products and the creation of design ideas and product innovations. For example the client is ready to get the latest software that meets his need to get beautiful digital images which have additional benefits for the client.

3.13   Marketing plan

It is important for the company to have a marketing strategy so that it can increase its productivity and be successful in the market. Most companies have developed at least 5 years of strategy plan to operate.

When the strategy is complete then tactics need to be developed to implement the company strategy, the tactic then focuses on the short term plan. This needs to be differentiated between strategic measurements and tactics.

Then when the company has a better understanding of the market places available to its customers and the unique position that the company has in the competitive market.

The management of the marketing company can get to make strategic decisions that are necessary, which in turn increases the productivity and profitability of the company. The decision making strategy is based on the specific goals and objectives of the company in the short term, this lead to the company's revenue growth, market share, long-term profitability or other targets.

Considering the strategic objectives of the company, the market focus, the desired market placement of the company, the brand of the product determined, and how best to implement the agreed strategy.

This then relates to 4 P's integrated marketing mix implementation planning. Product management, valuation, location (location or location of the product which can be local, regional, and national.

Implementing a marketing strategy is usually limited to 4 P's, also known as marketing mixed, which refers to the combination of business products that a company will use to implement a company's marketing strategy. The ultimate goal of market mixed is to regularly report and present a plan that enhances the placement chosen by the company.

As mentioned above all 4P's integrated marketing is the key to executing the company's marketing options. The overarching goals of the marketing mix are to place the company's choice, to build customer loyalty, and to strengthen the target customer brand based on the company's marketing and financial objectives.

The management of the marketing department will present a marketing plan to define the way the company will implement the selected strategies by identifying the planned strategy that the company aims to achieve in its business objectives. The marketing plans of the companies vary and the most important are the following:

Summary:

- Commentary on the situation to find out the real information and insights gained from market research and corporate marketing discussions.
- Present the company's objectives or long-term strategic plans.
- A statement relating to the essential objectives of the company, which include the marketing goals and financial projections of the company.
- The marketing strategy that the company has decided to adopt, outlining the areas of focus and competitive placement to achieve product implementation options in the marketing mix (4 P's)

3.14 Marketing Mix:

(UOP, 2020) As mentioned above the entrepreneur needs to understand the needs of the customers and deliver them to other business products and services in order to satisfy the needs of the customers.

Taking into account the above, the businessman should perform the following:

a. Produce products according to the needs of the customers.
b. that the products are available at a price that customers regard as reasonable and competitive.
c. delivering the products to the various customers of the company.
d. Consumers to receive information on the features and characteristics of the product utilizing through the media.

The marketing directors then make use of the four key decisions when planning for marketing activities known as Marketing mix items which are abbreviated as the four P's: (i) products, (ii) price, (iii) place (distribution location) and (iv) promotion. 4-tan 'P'

Marketing involves a variety of activities that are important to the company's business objectives. In order to be successful, the required commodity must be put on the market by delivering the appropriate commodity to the market. At the time that the customers need, and it is necessary to specify, distribute the goods, and determine the price of the goods, in order to be notified Customers that came to these products.

These four combined functions are called marketing mix or 4P's. If the business's marketing mix works well and the company made plans to attract customers and take advantage of the competitive market between companies of the same type or its counterpart to sell the same products or offer the similar services.

3.14.1 Products

A product refers to a products sold by a company or a service provided by a company, which in turn is intended to meet and satisfy the needs of the customers as well as meet the demands of the customers. It is then marketed after studies have found that it is needed in the market, and it is imperative that the products being marketed be considered and recognized as being different from others in the competitive market. The goods sold are not bought by the customer to own it only but also by the benefits of the purchased items, and should be lead to the satisfaction of the customers.

3.14.2 Price

The selling price of a product is also important and indicates the amount of money that customers want to spend on that business product or service. It is important that marketing officials pay close attention to the costs of research and development, production, marketing and distribution. It is also important to estimate the quality of the goods and the price of the goods or services on the market.

3.14.3 Placement

The goods or services are prepared for sale, so it is important that the goods are delivered in a convenient place where the customer can get them whenever he/she needs them.

The type of product features and characteristics are important when selling products, and it is necessary to decide where to place the goods when deciding where to sell the goods. We know that consumers have their own preferences and desires are very different, and the choice of product type depends on the customer's behavior, job title, financial status and level of social status.

Perhaps the clothes bought by a poor man with a very low income are different from those of purchased by a rich man. Inexpensive items can be found in many stores or warehouses, but expensive items can be found in a limited number of places or stores. It can be found in stores that are physically visible to customers or on the internet for pictures or the images and characters of the items.

3.14.4 Promotion:

When products are brought to market, it required to inform customers and launch a marketing campaign for a product or service to sell, which can be presented in an alternative way through social media such as mass media, social media, personal sales (mouth to mouth) or public relations system.

It is important that there is a specific budget to be reserved for the marketing. It is used by managers to promote integrated marketing services, especially branding, pricing and availability, which are called marketing mix or 3Ps. This is to reach the targeted customers, which is important to prepare a well-thought-out and concise message that summarizes the content to be conveyed in order to attract the attention of the targeted customers who's planned to reach the message.

3.15 International marketing:

(Luenendonk, M, 2019) International marketing we mean the process of improving the marketing strategies of companies that sell goods or services in foreign markets or in international markets outside the borders or operating in that company, so that the company can adapt and aligns with foreign countries outside its borders.

It involves the complete process of designing, creating, deploying and promoting a product or service that is intended to be delivered and sold in international markets.

In recent times, the advent of telecommunications, the Internet, and other media has made it easier for the world to come together, and it has made it possible for the international community to stay in touch with each other It looks that international community live only one village. As a result, the international community has reacted to the growing number of shocking events.

It also made it easier for businesses, most of which were operating locally or regionally, in order to establish business relationships.

Most large companies operate internationally, with offices and stores in the international market, and small companies are also taking advantage of the easy internet connection to make their products and services purchases global across borders. They used to work to reach customers around the world and sell their products.

As a result, many smaller companies are more likely to compete in the global marketplace in order to compete in the marketplace, which, if not encouraged by governments or business executives, may be left out of the market. As a result the markets of their countries compete with the big companies that are more economically, labor and professionally competent.

There are many rules and regulations governed by the World Trade Organization. There are the many laws that are being pushed by the economies of Europe and the United States who have developed policies to strengthen free market competition in the world and to facilitate world trade which is seen as much less important, take advantage of industrialized nations that sell their goods and services to poor third world countries in Africa, Asia and Latin America.

There are many benefits to international marketing when done correctly and as follows:

First, it can improve the quality of imported goods or services. This can enable the company to grow and develop as well as enhance the business market, they are preparing to produce products or provide new effective and quality services to attract new customers.

Secondly, the company is able to make a lot of profit from the competitive market competition, it is not a problem or it is easy for the companies to compete in the local markets, and there may be very few companies that still have significant success.

In the international trade market, then if your company is able to influence the business of the international trade market and your business competitors are not able to do so your company can be more profitable in market competition and more powerful than other local or international companies of the competition.

Thirdly, companies involved in global marketing are important to increase the advertising of their customers for your brand and the company's products or services, which make it cost-effective and can also boost your savings.

3.16 Marketing Management Pros and Cons:

Marketing is one of the most important aspects of business management, and marketing is a very interesting task but it is not easy to find the right strategy that can attract all the customers that the company planned to deliver its products and services to succeed from market competition.

To achieve this you need to constantly conduct regular surveys to measure the market needs of your customers and the performance and development of your business, and it is important to make your company have the necessary resources that are financially and professionally staffed, because Employees are the most important asset of a company.

It is important that the company is able to adapt to the challenges of the market, that it is important for you to be aware of the changes in the market and the new developments and to pay more attention to the idea of adding something new and always look for the right marketing mix and appropriate strategies to improve your company productivity, the tools you use, and keep up with the latest technology.

There has also been an increase in the number of digital advertisements on the internet, especially face books, you tube , what sup groups, telegrams, etc. have, and you are constantly updating so that it does not become boring.

3.16.1 Pros

If your company is one of the international traders you are one of the international marketers, you need to be active with more effort, knowledge and skills, which in turn creates a culture of learning from the world. and the diverse lifestyles of the international community and each customer to be informed in the most effective and simplest way possible, which can create a global and unique social culture.

The marketing process is influenced by the psychology and customer behavior of the customer, which requires you to study the different behaviors of the company's products, developing an advanced marketing plan based on the marking mix 4P's not above, We have talked about the importance of having a good market for your products and special business services.

- Strengthen the close relationship between the company and the customers so as to attract the attention of the customers so as to build the trust of different customers to be supportive of the company and a regular customer connected with the company.

- It is also important that your business, specially the strategies and tactics you use, be secured and not shared with anyone so that it does not attract competitors and you do not lose the free market competition.
- It is also important that you have access to data from other companies that are competing with you so that you can account it and add to your existing strategic and marketing plans.

The online advertising activity is called digital marketing. Digital marketing has become very popular in recent years, thanks to the ever changing technology and it seems that marketing is often becoming more digital. In comparison, the benefits of digital marketing outweigh the disadvantages.

Smriti, M 2021) Other major marketing benefits include the following:

(i) The importance of a business organization

One of the marketing advantages of a company is that it attracts marketers to satisfy the customer and sell it to meet the needs of the customer so that he can achieve the specific goals related to making a profit.

ii. Marketing allows customers to find products and services of their choice to meet their individual needs and desires. It creates productive benefits. Studies by marketers can help in deciding the product design, product characteristics, color, quantity and quality of products produced. Marketing also encourages the customer to make the final decision on the purchase.

iii. Marketing contributes to economic development

Marketing contributes to the economic development of the country or the world if the company operates in different countries of the world. We are aware that marketing activities create jobs and income, and in countries where trade contributes to the main sources of government revenue and taxes.

There are also public and private organizations and companies that directly and indirectly link their work or resources to advertising and marketing such as various media outlets and social media, publishing companies or transportation and revenue people who work.

(iv) Necessary for service companies and non-profit organizations:

There are many employees currently working in the service business. In most developed countries, most of the major sources of revenue are services related including telecommunications, healthcare, entertainment, education, financial services, taxation and other consulting services.

3.16.2   Cons

Marketing is not the easy thing to conduct and it requires knowledge, skills and experience, so when making a selection of marketing staff you need to recruit the right people who can perform the job well, and the organization to provide ongoing personal training and development to have the required knowledge in house, It is important that employees are good at communicating and socializing, and that they can earn the trust of the customers.

Some marketers do not have a good reputation in the consumer or in the community, who are seen as liars who exaggerate their own interests and the interests of the companies and not the interests of the customers and the society.

Marketer's salaries are often very low compared to other departments such as the sales or logistics department and are not paid well enough, which is often unsatisfactory and has very low motivation which could be impacted growth and development and overall success of the company.

- Most people outside the company are unaware of the importance of marketing, the important work that marketers perform and the actual work they do for the company. It is important for the employer to try to make customers understand what is the marketing work is and how important it is for marketers and customers to have a very close relationship.

3.17 Summery:

Marketing management is the organizational behavior of a company in which organizations or companies study how best to get their business to the market and how best to conduct marketing orientation, most relevant messages and media resources to find out and monitor and respond to market customers' responses.

Marketing management also helps the company operate the financial resources and create a competitive strategy to discuss the formal business model of the company. Sometimes a marketing strategy focuses on a specific customer who sends them messages or ads to arouse and attract their attention.

Another strategy that influences the marketing of a business is the competition of the stock market, which deals with popular brands and the use of price strategies to then attract the attention of customers who are interested in that particular business. Take, for example, Microsoft and Apple. Microsoft handles data, texting, soft data and emails making it the most productive and commercially viable.

Marketing is really about understanding and recognizing the needs of people and society and how to meet these needs which include different areas of individual and social needs such as food, shelter, clothing, transportation etc. There is also a need to create new and emerging needs, in order to increase productivity.

Key concepts in marketing include understanding and meeting the needs, desires and demands of the market to be focused.

As mentioned above the entrepreneur needs to understand the needs of the customers and deliver them to other business products and services in order to satisfy the needs of the customers.

Needs are something that satisfies the basic needs of the customer or human being. Desire is the wishes or demand for specific products or services that a person needs. Orders are specific products that the customer is willing or able to pay for or purchase.

International marketing we mean the process of improving the marketing strategies of companies that sell goods or services in foreign markets or in international markets outside the borders or operating in that company, so that the company can adapt and aligns with foreign countries outside its borders.

It involves the complete process of designing, creating, deploying and promoting a product or service that is intended to be delivered and sold in international markets.

In recent times, there has been an increase in the number of large companies, mostly multilateral companies, operating outside of their home country and trading in many countries around the world. In recent years, there have also been small companies operating internationally.

3.18 Recommendations:

Marketing is the most important part of a company or company so that it can be successful in the business market. Improving marketing is therefore essential for the economic growth and business development of a company.

In order to achieve the company's goals it is important that the marketing department of the company conducts market research so that it can understand and satisfy wants and needs of the customers. And there is a need to study the correct customer attitudes and behaviors that are not based on assumptions.

In addition, the marketing department needs the marketing team to have the tools and resources they need to succeed in their marketing related tasks, and they need to work with and adapt to modern technologies such as the use of digital equipment. .

It is also advisable to set up a special marketing team such as a marketing committee with a business intelligence unit to assist a company in obtaining market information and other companies that are competing with their strategic strategy.

Coolman, A, 2017). It is also a good idea for the marketing team to focus on the following:

1. Perform a cross department workflow.
2. Keep your audience in mind
3. Know your customers
4. Adjust all customer feedback.
5. Establish key marketing standards.
6. Prioritize content.
7. Stay tuned.
8. Focus on the Return on Investment strategy(ROI) of your campaign.
9. Implement the Lean method to find out which campaigns work.
10. Use the Scrum tab to focus on weekly priorities.
11. Keep experimenting with new marketing methods.
12. Develop a long-term marketing plan.
13. Hire a strategic analyst
14. Continue to manage customer data.
15. Remain Accountable.

3.19 Bibliography:

- (Coolman, A, 2017), Improve your marketing operation: online available: https://www.wrike.com/blog/improve-your-marketing-operations. Retrieved on 15-12-2021.

- (Smriti, M 2021) 5 major advantages of marketing: onlin available https://www.yourarticlelibrary.com/marketing/5-major-advantages-of-marketing/27962, retrieved- 10-12-2021

- (Luenendonk, M, 2019) , Global marketing strategy onlineavailable;**https://www.cleverism.com/global-marketing-strategies/retrived 25-11-2021**.

- (UOP, 2020) Marketing mix, online available: http://www.uop.edu.pk/ocontents/marketing%20mix.pdf, retrieved 12-12-2021.
- **(CGMA, 2021) Cost Transformation Model online available. https://www.cgma.org/resources/tools/cost-transformation-model/kotlers-five-product-level-model.html,** retrieved 02-12-2021.

- Cimorelli, T(2021) kotlers five productleve model.html, available online: https://www.cgma.org/resources/tools/cost-transformation-model/kotlers-five-product-level-model.html. retrieved 02-12-2021
- (*Morgen*, W ,*6 August2003*). "*First Among Marketers*". *Financial Times.*
- (SHARMA, 2015), what are marketing management task,online available: https://www.slideshare.net/101iiminternship/what-are-the-marketing-management-tasks-49558791, retrieved 22-12-2021.
- (Indeed, 2021), Marketing planning objectives: https://www.indeed.com/career-advice/career-development/marketing-planning-objectives. Retrieved on 22-2021.
-
- (Išoraitė, 20014) file:///C:/Users/User/AppData/Local/Temp/6094140.pdf

Chapter Four:

4.   Consumer's behavior

4.1 Introduction:

(*Bray*, J. P., 2008) Consumer decision-making processes have a long history of more than 300 years of history, initiated by former economists led by experts such as Nicholas Bernoulli. John von Neumann and Oskar Morgenstern, and are believed to have started consumer decision making (Richarme 2007) with a focus on economics, and were then interested in purchasing. This concept is known as the Utility Theory.

This is to determine the customer's choice of the final product. This approach makes it clear that consumers are making sensible decisions that are concerned about their personal interests in the pursuit of their own Interests.

Various studies later conducted by other scholars have changed the utility theory to study these issues in order to find out more than the different consumer behaviors.

The concept of consumer's behavior in the marketing has become important from a variety of perspectives, and it is a new field of study in various science departments including economics, psychology, sociology, anthropology and marketing science related to business management.

From a marketing perspective, customer behavior has become an important field of learning through the concept of marketing.

In order to implement the concepts of the marketing it is necessary to look specifically at the production and distribution of goods that can cover the small needs and the diversity of goods and services in the market, and then there was great progress in the 1950s in terms economy.

After World War II, marketing ideas became very strong due to the lack of formal demand. There has been an economic downturn which has reduced consumer spending capacity, which is seen as a result of a lack of interest in consumers' behavior.

At the same time, with less competition in the manufacturing sector, the product can be quickly marketed and sold.

The current marketing method according to Schiffman & Kanuk (1997) is called production orientation, and we have since followed the marketing process. They tried to sell the products they wanted which they produce on their own.

At that time consumers were reluctant to buy the product actively, until companies or marketers came under intense pressure to buy the products, which then does not take into account the satisfaction of customers buying.

This has led to surveys in order to understand customer behavior, needs, purchasing power and interest in existing customers' desire, access, and sales.

4.2 Customer orientation

The perspective of positive criticism of a product helps companies that marketers adapt to produce new production to adapt and meet the diverse needs of customers at a rapid pace of changes.

It is important that companies are successful in the business market, as many companies change their marketing policies, with their products based on customer needs.

There are a total of three aspects to the consumer's understanding of market trends and the process of innovation and development.

And now the marketing system works for the customers system is the driver of the existing strategy and marketing decision. At present the strategy is not developed until an assessment is done from different angles including the type of product itself. Production and marketing are driven by future customer needs.

It is true that many products have failed despite the development of research and technological studies that have shown that they are needed at that time.

The most popular form of marketing that focuses on customers is called Solution, information and accessibility. This system is generally converted into the four P's used to develop the client's attention span. These are (Product, Promotion, Price, and Place of Marketing Management.

Assael (1995: 5) focuses on the relationship of marketing concept that needs to be understood first the benefits of companies looking for a market where customers can access their diverse needs, followed by the development of marketing plans that meet customer needs.

(Walters, 1974) gave consumer behavior the following definition: the process by which an individual seeks or determines what, when, where, how and by whom the goods or services are to be purchased.

(Mowen, 1993) describes the consumer involved in the acquisition, use and disposal of goods, services, experiences and concepts, expanded to include not only the individual but also groups who buy specific goods or services. This then means more than just the customer or the purchase.

Schiffman & Kanuk (1997) scholars describe consumer culture as: "The culture in which consumers present the search, purchase, use, evaluation, and disposal of goods, services, and ideas."

We can then define consumer behavior when buying something as a study of consumer behaviors that can affect when people want to make decisions about the partner or service they want to buy that meet their needs, contact with a product, service or company.

It is therefore very important to understand the behavior and attitudes of customers as they will respond to a new product or service in the market and the experience and expertise learned from those already familiar with the market.

When it comes to researching consumer behavior, it is important to know how individuals make the decisions they make with the purchase of goods or services they buy with a time, money, and effort), which then studies why, when, where and how often they buy and how they use what was bought.

Then we can say that customer behavior generally focuses on the behaviors that customers display in searching, buying, using, evaluating and other behaviors related to the use, evaluation and disposal of goods and services they deem to be able to meet their needs.

If then one of the four Ps is in disarray or not one of the key elements of a business marketing strategy, it is at risk of a catastrophic event that could lead to a recession.

However, in recent years the marketing service has expanded to be considered 7P in marketing, and the following four factors have been added: Physical Environment, and People.

Schiffman & Kanuk (1997) the two leading experts in this field also believe that there are two groups when it comes to consumer behavior: individual customers and the group or team of the organization.

When customers make a purchase, they buy the items individually when buying furniture or as a gift in the form of a gift for an individual. Assess whether there may be advantages or disadvantages in terms of companies or organizations, government agencies and existing agencies. Understanding customer behavior also helps companies or organizations identify opportunities in the market that are not yet covered.

An example of consumer behavior was focused on dietary habits associated with gluten-free (GF) product needs. The companies that studied the changes in the consumer diet have created GF products to then meet the market opportunities and the constant or changing needs of the customers.

And there are many companies that do not follow the culture and understanding of the needs and desires of the customers, which has led some companies to develop in terms of customer competition in the market.

4.3 General Analysis OF Consumers behavior.

(Write pass Journal, 20120) When customers want to make a purchase, they first go through a process based on a series of steps, which is to first find out what the need is and then think about how to meet that need.

They look for information to meet that need, then find the right solution, evaluate that and then look at whether there is another solution, and then make the right decision to buy in order to own the product or service they need.

When the client is in the data search system, the information retrieval system, the psychological object of the customer is the concept that affects the way the customer receives that information which is also related to the customer's source of information and how the customer is satisfied.

Customer presumption is the foundation of a marketing program, which is used for a variety of communication and emotional stimulation including images, speech or listening, text, color, noise, music, taste and smell.

In order to cover this and strengthen the communication campaign related to information retrieval, it must have information or informative behaviors. It is their job to show marketers the unique customer attitudes and characteristics.

This can create brand awareness, which creates a trusting environment that eliminates stress and suspicion surrounding products and customers and facilitates awareness campaigns or advertisements.

Consumer opinion is always unique and has unparalleled potential, which is why the consumer decides to buy a product after he or she is satisfied with the benefits he or she will receive from the product and is able to meet the needs that the customer buys a particular product or service and sacrifices his property.

It is therefore important for the marketer to understand the customer's unique views and desires so that he or she can be successful in convincing the customer.

Consumers regularly receive advertising campaigns for the product, so that the concept of choice is part of the customer's perception process, enabling the cognitive process to examine some of the stimuli that may influence a customer's decision to purchase a product.

This is important for the marketer to come up with a clear advertising strategy, and it is best to bring a test copy to the market first to make sure customers understand the message, and it is important that you do not use the wrong message or image instead of driving company business. Things to look out for include jokes, exaggerations and anything that may come back to haunt you.

Also note that the customer's perception and understanding is unique, and people do not share the same views and sympathizing ,everyone has their own views and comprehension, and the way customers interpret and perceiving advertising information may vary, and Someone may take your advertising message from a different perspective than you intended it, and it is important that you regularly monitor the perception and vision of the advertising message so that you can take stock of it and learn from it.

The customers's way of understanding or interpreting depends on the client's knowledge, experience of the client's feelings. And there may be differences in the customer's perception and reality which can lead to an understanding environment in which the customer decides to buy the spesific product or stop using your business services. Maintaining communication and continuation of understanding between the business and the customer is important.

(Bray, J. P., 2008) The consumer is a human being so in order to understand customer behavior, it is appropriate to understand Human behavior. Human behavior can be defined as the ability of responses and the way in which these powers manifest themselves in relation to individuals or groups of people to respond to stimuli or experiences from internal and external factors during their lifetime.

Human behavior focuses on the way people behave and how they respond to events and changes in their environment and relationships. It is based on a number of factors such as the influence of a person's culture, norms, values and attitudes.

Human behavior is related to the different behaviors expressed by human beings in relation to culture, behaviors, emotions, values, ethics, management, relationships, persuasion, coercion and / or culture and things that vary from person to group and create a variety of actions or behaviors that affect everyone.

Kotler (Gould, 1979), says that it is difficult to do when it reveals why society or consumers are buying things as there are different things that affect the human brain that cause the human being to eventually responds by buying directly based on what the person or group of the organization needs.

Runyon & Stewart (1987) define the concept of human interaction, which focuses on theories held about human behavior, and influences their behavior, so it is normal to look at this system of behavior by from a variety of perspectives including economic perspectives, which marketers want to have an economic impact on by encouraging the sale of a product or services.

It is also possible to look at issues from a social perspective, which marketers use to look at human behaviors related to the individual, family, community or organization, references and social values. Factors influencing customer behavior in marketing aspects:

In order to better understand customer behavior in relation to marketing, it is very important to understand these three factors including culture, customers in psychological, personal and social aspects.

4.3 1 Psychological issues:

Consumers' lives and behavior are affected by a variety of factors related to their way of thinking. Psychological issues may include the perception of a need or situation and the ability of a person to learn or understand that information and the individual's behavior, and each client may respond to the marketing message related to their thinking and behavior.

It is a good idea for marketers to take these psychological factors into account when making marketing campaign messages and to pay attention to whether their campaign may attract the attention of their target audience.

There is also the theory of human psychology based on a holistic view that then focuses on the whole person (Holism), which looks at human behavior in relation to the observer's point of view and attention, but also the emphasis on behaviors and personal attitudes.

4.3.2 Personal Issues (Privacy).

Personal issues are personal characteristics that may not be in direct contact with others but with the client or the individuals.

These goals may include individual decisions, personal habits, interests and perspectives, with special considerations in mind. The decisions one makes can also affect one's age, gender, background, temperament and other personal circumstances.

For example, an older person may have different behaviors than a young person, which can affect the choice and decision making process. And young people may be more in need than adults and can spend more on items they didn't need at the time.

Perhaps the style of choice for adults and young people is very different and there are enough examples of different outfits and other things related to the entertainment business that young and old are not the same.

4.3.3 Social Issues

The third factor that can have a significant impact on society in relation to customer behavior is social behavior.

Client influences on social issues may include family, social relationships, the workplace or school or any person or group associated with that client.

Social factors can also affect a person's income, living conditions, education level and role in society. It is also important to understand that social factors and the impact of consumer behavior on marketing are not easy to analyze when developing marketing plans.

Yet there is no doubt that the importance of social issues in terms of customer behavior should be taken into account as it has no effect on how the community responds to marketing and makes purchasing decisions such as employment, a popular spokesperson who can have a significant impact on buyers and persuade them to buy products and use special services.

4.4 How Consumers behavior applies to reality.

(Grimsley, Sh, 2015) Consumer purchasing behavior is the sum total of decisions Tradition aggregates the total consumer, preferences, objectives, and position related to the consumer behavior in the market when purchasing a product or service.

The study of client behavior is related to anthropology, psychology, sociology and economics. This practice consists of various systems including the following.

1. The customer recognizes the problem. The first step is for the client to identify the problem. He acknowledges that she has an unmet need. For example, if the refrigerator gets out of order, you will not have enough money to buy a new one. The customer realizes that she now needs to borrow or buy a second hand refrigerator instead.

2. Searching for information. The second step is for the customer to seek information about the products they need so that they can solve the problem.

3. Assessment: the client then evaluates the information received based on the customer's needs, preferences and available resources. For example, the customer will limit his choice to buy a new refrigerator in three different sizes, and buy a second refrigerator that has several options.

Based on the price, quality of the refrigerator, and the volume and length of the refrigerator, you can also look at the fire it can use and how appropriate it is for the home or storage space and the lighting equipment it uses.

4. Purchasing: At this stage the customer makes the final decision regarding the sale of the refrigerator. We wanted to buy the best and most suitable refrigerator that could meet his need as a special refrigerator because its price was the best he could negotiate, and it was immediately available.

5. After the sale price at this stage, the customer will decide whether he is satisfied with the sale of this refrigerator. That way the buyer will be happy to buy this item. If he is not satisfied, why not? This last step is important for recurring sales; once the customer is satisfied with the item he has bought he will buy again from there.

4.4.1 Factors that influence consumer buying behavior.

1. These include cultural, social, personal, psychological and economic factors.

2. Personality

Schiffman (2008) described how a person's unique dynamics, both physical and mental, are influenced by the behaviors and responses of the social and physical environment, which are related to heritage, the environment in which he or she was raised and the childhood experiences.

 3. Psychological activities are also influenced by physical activities such as the client's interests and perceptions.

4. Influenced by the family: The family helps shape one's attitudes and actions to develop political and religious views, lifestyle choices, and consumer wants and demands.

5. A society beyond the influence of others

6. Behavior and way of life "the way people live and spend time and money." Faith and emotion

7. The Value of Vision • Organization, • Recognition, • Interpretation

8. Organize, identify and interpret emotional information to represent and understand the environment. It can be shaped by learning, memory and expectations.

4.4.2 Consumers behaviour Pros and cons of the topic on a local, national and international level

(Hammond, K, 2017) Marketing professionals study customer behavior so that they understand their behavior, and sometimes present decorated stories using negative style or patterns, and also help to market the product by no facilities or discounts.

The customer is bathed in the results or recommendations of the study including where to buy things. Customers can get extra bucks that allow them to buy products at a discount or at a much lower price. It can also have a disadvantage associated with taking items that cost a lot of money and spending more on items that might customer are not the first priorities.

Studies conducted by merchants in relation to consumer's behavior have shown that customers' behaviors and specific needs vary. We have found that not all customers buy by regulating the price or use of a product that he or she has experienced and used in the past.

In particular, the upper class and lower class of workers have different shopping habits, and it may be bought by rich people for prestige, reputation or performance. Such perceptions related to purchasing behaviors contradict conventional consumer behaviors related to economics and purchasing.

There are private shops or companies that then target the upper class merchants who need special products and services that need to be taken into account and understand their own needs that may be different from other regular customers.

4.4.3. Advantages:

Benefits of understanding customer behavior

• meeting customer needs
• They can learn or understand customer behavior
• The customer is informed and compares the products and their prices so that they can choose the products on the market.
• The entrepreneur makes sure that the customer decides to buy from his or her shop.
• Traders can also check whether the customer is satisfied with the product they have purchased.
• Entrepreneurs can use customer feedback for future development and innovation.

Purchasing Comparison

Consumers can compare and contrast different stores, which differ in brand name and style. This comparison can lead to market competition which in turn can lead to lower customer prices to attract customers and sell more products, and also give consumers the opportunity to choose between different products.

The final decision

Another benefit for consumers is that they have the right to make the final decision to make a purchase. The final decision on the purchase depends on the customer only, which is why retailers, especially those in stores, should try to influence customer behavior so that they can make the final decisions.

Advertising Effects

Advertising is the best way for merchants to influence purchases, ads that can then attract customers to be used for successful advertising and then increase customer interest and desire.

Entrepreneurs use advertising messages to then study the creation of a search for specific needs of customers.

4.4.3 Disadvantages :Limited resources:

There is wisdom that a Somali man from the countryside who came to a big city with a small amount of money entered a shop with a wide variety of goods. When he saw that each of them needed his family and that he had little money and the need for the goods in the shop that his family needed, he said, "O Allah, what are a goods does my family need in the shop? Who will give me money to buy it?

Advertising messages that companies send to customers, in turn, affect the customer's marketing behavior, which can lead to customers accepting or responding to advertisements and having a limited amount of money forcing advertisers to buy the advertised products, it Some may not have needed it at the time but it was not the first priority of the item in the purchasing plan but the advertising campaign message pressured it to outperform those who had previously purchased the item. As a result, he may seek a loan to buy the goods and then fall into the debt trap that the customer falls into when making purchasing decisions in order to meet their needs.

Marketers want to know the customer's attitude towards buying so they can plan their products, and sometimes they deliver beautiful messages with negative concepts. Advertising and marketing messages to consumers through the media can greatly arouse consumer sentiment. They take full advantage of the loopholes and areas where customers are vulnerable and tell them that the product has any excess or tell them that they have made a discount so that they can rush and buy the product through the exchange system, gifts, lottery and ohers.

For example, some traders have argued that toothpaste decreases and protects the risk of tooth decay or mouth infection.

Major pharmaceutical companies tell consumers that they can cure many diseases, and instead tell them what are the the side effective of the medicine.

There are also special offers for expensive products that merchants take advantage of to attract customers by changing the style of packaging, decoration and branding, which may not be of better quality than similar products in the market for low prices, but it is confusing and playful with the customer's intelligence.

4.5 Conclusions

Katyab, D(2019) There is an international wisdom saying that the customer is king, so the customer is very important in the business because he/she is the one who depends on the final decision on the purchase. The customer then determines the required demand, so in order for the procurement process to be successful it is necessary to understand the behaviors and characteristics of this person making the decisions, which in turn are influenced by a variety of factors including social, economic, cultural and even the climate of the area at that time.

Decisions are also influenced by the client's level of education, the customer's level of economic development and location, and can also affect the client's lifestyle, information and additional information about the consumer's products, care, family size and other similar issues.

Then learning about customer behaviors is useful for why customers or groups from different sections of society respond or make decisions at different stages related to the flow, purchase, or disposal of goods and services that include existing or ongoing decision-making processes

(Writepass Jounal, 2012) We have focused this study on consumer behavior, which we have mentioned that marketing staff should before conducting advertisements first study consumer behavior related to shopping, customers are human beings so to do that It is important to understand human behavior and its implications and how that impact can be exploited so that markets or products sold by traders can be marketed. It is very important that there is a close relationship and understanding between both the buyer and the seller.

When it comes to researching consumer behavior, it is important to know how individuals make the decisions they make with the purchase of goods or services they buy with a time, money, and effort), which then studies why, when, where and how often they buy and how they use what was bought.

When customers want to make a purchase, they first go through a process based on a series of steps, which is to first find out what the need is and then think about how to meet that need.

They look for information to meet that need, then find the right solution, evaluate that and then look at whether there is another solution, and then make the right decision to buy in order to own the product or service they need.

Then we can say that customer behavior generally focuses on the behaviors that customers display in searching, buying, using, evaluating and other behaviors related to the use, evaluation and disposal of goods and services they deem to be able to meet their needs.

If then one of the four Ps is in disarray or not one of the key elements of a business marketing strategy, it is at risk of a catastrophic event that could lead to a recession.

As mentioned above, consumer perceptions and behaviors seem to be very close to each other, both of which are based on influencing customer perceptions. In order to understand the customer's interpretation and the attitudes, we have described the most influential understanding and behavior related to the customer's purchasing behavior.

We have focused on understanding how to develop these concepts in order to better understand different customer behaviors, and different perspectives and examples have been suggested so that marketers can take advantage of this and get grasp of the behaviors customers engagement, to then prepare the most appropriate marketing strategy and how to then deliver the right message to the customers.

Studies conducted by merchants in relation to the consumers behavior have shown that customers' behaviors and specific needs vary. We have found that not all customers buy by regulating the price or use of a product that he or she has experienced and used in the past.

In particular, the upper class and lower class of workers have different shopping habits. It may be bought by rich people for prestige, reputation or performance. Such perceptions related to purchasing behaviors contradict conventional consumer behaviors related to economics and purchasing.

There are private shops or companies that then target the upper class merchants who need special products and services that need to be taken into account and understand their own wants and needs that may be different from other regular customers.

4.6 Suggestion and Recommendations

There is a need to understand the behavior and preferences of the customers, and it is important to research the different behaviors of the customers and make them central and thoughtful when developing a marketing plan for different products, in order to increase and encourage that customers are satisfied with the purchase of the product they want in order to get it and use it, then the messages sent to the customer should be given serious consideration to encourage him to make a decision and buy the goods held by the trader.

In addition, the customer is better served by contacting or visiting the company's stores or services, and it is a good idea for the business community to take advantage of this and welcome customers with open arms and the appropriate behavior of your very intentions.

I find that customer satisfaction stimulates understanding of customer behavior so that it becomes a free advertisement.

• Strengthen perspectives on new positive customer behavior to build understanding between entrepreneur and customer.
• Planning emerging trends to create new product and delivery opportunities that motivate the customer.
• Maintain new behaviors through a general understanding of the client and his or her behavior.
• The customer's messages should reach the customer's mind, and the customer should be able to understand the message better in simple language and not in an in formal or literary way.
• It is also important that marketers and marketers comment on and understand the perceptions of consumer behavior so that they can influence the decision to buy.

4.7 Bibliography

Assael, H. (1995). Consumer Behavior and Marketing Action. South-Western College Publishing.

Bray, J. P., 2008) Consumer Behaviour Theory: Approaches and Models, onlineavailable: https://www.academia.edu/37401396/Consumer_Behaviour_Theory_Approaches_and_Models, accessed on 25-10-2021

Ethical Consumer, (2008) Consumer Boycotts. [Internet] Available from: <http://www.ethicalconsumer.org/Boycotts/aboutboycotts.aspx> [Accessed 10 April 2011]

(Grimsley, Sh, 2015) What Is Consumer Buying Behavior? Retrieved from https://study.com/academy/lesson/what-is-consumer-buying-behavior-definition-types-quiz.html.accessed 20-10-2021.

(Hammond, K, 2017, advantages and disadvantages consumers: retrieved from https://bizfluent.com/info-8711517-advantages-disadvantages-consumer.html. accessed 23-10-2021

RICHARME, M., 2-6-7. Consumer Decision-Making Models, Strategies, and Theories, Oh My!, [online].Available from www.decisionanalyst.com/Downloads/ConsumerDecisionMaking.pdf [Accessed: 2-6-7]. SCHIFFMAN, L. G. , et al., 2007.

Schiffman & Kanuk (1997), Consumer behaviour, Pearson Prentice Hall, 2007

Mowen, J. C. *1993*. Consumer Behavior. Third Edition. Macmillan Publishing. Company. New York. Olson, J. C., & Reynolds, T. J .

Walters, 1974, "Organizational Behavior - Human Behavior at work", 9th edition New Delhi: Tata McGraw Hil

Writepass Journal, 2012), consumer behaviour theory and practice, onlineavailebale:https://writepass.com/journal/2012/11/consumer-behaviour-theory-and-practice/, accessed- 21-10-2021.

Katyab, D(2019). Retrieved from https://www.yourarticlelibrary.com/consumer-behaviour/consumer-behaviour-meaning-factor-advantages-and-disadvantages. accessed on 15-10-2012

Jim Blythe, (1997) **The Essence of Consumer Behaviour**. London, Prentice Hall.

Solomon, M., G. Bamossy, S. Askegaard and M. Hogg (2009) **Consumer Behaviour: A European Perspective**. FT Prentice Hall (4th Edition).

Dickinson, R., and S.C. Hollander, **Consumer Votes**, Journal of Business Research, Vol.23, No.1, 9-20.

Hazem Jamjourm, (2008) **BDS & The Global Anti-Apartheid Movement.** Badil Resource Resource Center.

Rob Harrison, Terry Newholm, Deirdre Shaw, (2005) **The Ethical Consumer**. London, Sage Publications Ltd.

The Economist (1990), **Boycotting Corporate America**, The Economist, May 26, 69-70.

Dolliver, M. (2000). **Boomers as boycotters**. Adweek, (Eastern edn), 12 April, 44.

Manheim, J. B. (2001) **The death of a thousand cuts: Corporate campaigns and the attack on the corporation.** Mahwah, NJ: Lawrence Erlbaum.

Smith, N. Craig (1990), **Morality and the Market: Consumer Pressure for Corporate Accountability**, London: Routledge.

Friedman, M. (1999). **Consumer Boycotts**, New York: Routledge.

Laidler, H. (1968). **Boycotts and the Labor Struggle: Economic and Legal Aspects**, New York: Russell and Russell.

Baumeister, Roy F. (1998), **"The Self," in Handbook of Social Psychology**, Daniel T. Gilbert, Susan T. Fiske and Gardner Lindzey ed. Boston: McGraw-Hill.

Pittman, Thane S. (1998), **"Motivation," in Handbook of Social Psychology**, Daniel T. Gilbert, Susan T.Fiske and Gardner Lindzey ed. Boston: McGraw-Hill.

Friedman, M. (1985). **Consumer boycotts in the United States, 1970–1980: contemporary events in historic perspective**. Journal of Consumer Affairs, 19, 98–117.

Garrett, Dennis E. (1987), **"Effectiveness of Marketing Policy Boycotts: Environmental Opposition to Marketing,"** Journal of Marketing 54 (April), pp. 46-57.

International Monetary Fund, (2010) **World Economic Outlook Report**. [Internet] Available from: < http://www.imf.org/external/ns/cs.aspx?id=28> [Accessed 12 April 2011]

Jim Blythe, (2001) **Essentials of Marketing**. London, Prentice Hall.

William D.Wells and David Prensky, (1996) **Consumer Behavior**. New York, John Wiley & Sons, Inc.

Sak Onkvisit and John J. Shaw, **Consumer Bahaviour, Strategy and Analysis** (New York: Macmillan, 1994).

D. Krech and R. Crutchfield, **Theory and Problems in Social Psychology**, McGraw-Hill, New York, 1948.

Michael R. Solomon, (2004) **Consumer Behaviou: buying, having, and being**. London, Prentice Hall.

Jim Blythe, (2008) **Essentials of Marketing**. London, Prentice Hall.

Martin Fishbein (1963), **An investigation of the Relationship Between Beliefs About an Object and the Attitude Toward That Object**, *Human Relations*, 16, 233 – 240.

Terence A. Shimp (1981), **Attitude toward the Ad as a Mediator of Consumer Brand Choice**, *Journal of Advertising*, 10 (2), 9-15 ff.

Katiba, G., and B. Strumpel. (1978) **A New Economic Era.** New York: Elsevier.

CHAPTER FIVE:

5.   Human Resources Management:

5.1 Introduction;

Human Resource Management is the process of recruiting, developing and training the staff, compensating and evaluating employees, participating in their working relationships, safety, security and health and worrying about it.

HRM is a comprehensive work and management activity related to the recruitment, development and protection of employees, which in turn affects the overall work performance of the organization, which can lead to the organization achieving its goals and objectives.

HRM is the study of activities related to the people working in the organization. It is the responsibility of the administration to work to meet the needs of the organization in terms of the skills and abilities of the employees.

We can define HRM as the management of recruitment and promotion and care for the people working in the organization and the workforce focuses on the employees working in the organization.

HRM was established as a management system to ensure that human talent is used, efficiently and effectively to achieve the organization's goals.

In other words, HRM is a staff office responsible for recruiting, developing, compensating, integrating and caring for the organization's staff, which aims to help the organization achieve its specific goals.

Personnel management is therefore the planning, organizing, directing and monitoring of the performance of those who perform the tasks being performed (Edward B. Philippo).

According to Invancevich and Glueck experts, HRM focuses on the most efficient and effective use of human resources to achieve the specific goals and objectives of the organization.

It is a way of managing how people in the organization work or play a lion's share in doing the work that awaits the organization.

Dessler (2008) states that the practice policy related to the performance of human resource management applies to the activities, policies, and practices associated with obtaining, implementing, utilizing, evaluating and maintaining the best number and integrated skills of the workforce to fulfill the objectives of the organization.

The HRM policy is designed to guide the workflow process, such as improving the relationship between staff and the organization in order to achieve the desired goal. Employees are the engine that drives the work, so they need to be satisfied with the work they do which is a measure of the organization's HRM policy.

As employees are the most important foundation of the organization, it is important that employees are happy with the work they are performing, so that employees can engage, increase motivation, remain loyal and enhance work performance. At end I would like to investigate the impact of HRM policy on employee satisfaction.

The objectives of HRM policy include: producing high-quality and satisfying work, as well as self confidence, and employees should feel that the work is appropriate for their abilities and knowledge and that they are treated well and fairly and it is true that when employees are happy with the work they automatically manafacture more productivity.

Managing employee job satisfaction is one of the most important and challenging issues facing managers of the companies at the moment, and it is important that the organization has clear HRM policies so that employees are satisfied and happy with the policy for the organization or company they work for.

5.2   Back ground history:

Human Resources Management has gone through various stages related to different periods of its existence. Labour forces have been a need for employers since the settlement of the pastoralists and agriculture. It was originally called manpower, personal management, and is now called Human Resources Management (HRM).

The process began with recruiting people to work with the others, such as selling the people like commodity. The worker did not take what he earned but had to get food and shelter.

The legal and human rights system began during the Babylonian civilization under the leadership of King Humrawi.

There was a time when modern history began to think about the rights of workers in the European industrial revolution that took place in the early 18th century. When the machinery industry emerged, skilled workers were needed. At that time the workers began to complain about their long hours and very low wages.

The personal management began in the United States in 1901 when companies were organized to set up a special department for employees. This changed dramatically at the beginning of the First World War, when most men were involved in the war, and labour was needed, allowing women to be employed in certain occupations.

In order to find a solution to the labor issue, the International Labor Organization (ILO) was formed after the end of the war in 1919. HRM started in the United States in the second half of the world and went live in the 1950s, but the UK and the rest of Europe went straight to the 1980s.

There is now a perception that the staff is the most important asset of the organization, which in order for the organization to achieve its goals. It is necessary to have a skilled workforce who receive training to enhance their skills, encouraging personal development and providing the care they require to meet their needs so that the organization to achieve its planned goals.

The organization is to focus the employees being satisfied with the work they are doing for the organization and participating when the important decisions in the organization are being taken.

The current HRM functions are including planning and organizing, directing and controlling the staff to perform their jobs, and controls the activities of the outside or need work or are not moving staff, recruitment of staff, selection and employees placement of personnel and placement of movement of workers, training and implementation skills planning.

The HRM Department duties are including the planning and promotion of staffing, rewards and compensation and staff compensation. Designing and streamlining work schedules encouraging and evaluating work performance, reward management and boosting morale and maintenance services.

The HRM department also liaises with the trade unions, and deals with trade union and trade bargaining, decision-making and contractual agreement with the relevant parties 'unions and employers' unions. The HRM department also conducts staff registration, research and employee supervision during working hours and management of work stays and vacations.

In other words, HRM is a staff office responsible for recruiting, developing, compensating, integrating and caring for the organization's staff, which aims to help the organization achieve its specific goals.

Personnel management is therefore the planning, organizing, directing and monitoring of the performance of those who perform the tasks being performed. (Edward B. Philippo).

According to Invancevich and Glueck (1989) experts, HRM focuses on the most efficient and effective use of human resources to achieve the specific goals and objectives of the organization.It is a way of managing how people in the organization work or play a lion's share in doing the work that awaits the organization.

Dessler (2008) states that the practice policy related to the performance of human resource management applies to the activities, policies, and practices associated with obtaining, implementing, utilizing, evaluating and maintaining the best number and integrated skills of the workforce to fulfill the objectives of the organization.

The HRM policy is designed to guide the workflow process, such as improving the relationship between staff and the organization in order to achieve the desired goal. Employees are the engine that drives the work, so they need to be satisfied with the work they do which is a measure of the organization's HRM policy.

As employees are the most important foundation of the organization, it is important that employees are happy with the work they are performing, so that employees can engage, increase motivation, remain loyal and enhance work performance. At end I would like to investigate the impact of HRM policy on employee satisfaction.

The objectives of HRM policy include: producing high-quality and satisfying work, as well as self-confidence, and employees should feel that the work is appropriate for their abilities and knowledge and that they are treated well and fairly. And it is true that when employees are happy with the work they automatically produce more productivity.

Managing employee job satisfaction is one of the most important and challenging issues facing managers of the companies at the moment, and it is important that the organization has clear HRM policies so that employees are satisfied and happy with the policy for the organization or company they work for.

5.3 Current Human Resources Management:

The 21st century (Advancement human resources management) saw the emergence of human resource management and the management of human capital). Due to the increase in technology and knowledge based industrial production there is an increase in global trade competition. It was found that there was only a handful of staff with the right skills required.

There has been an increase in the number of organizations and companies interested in the management of human resources so that companies can achieve their goals and have greater respect for the value of their work in relation to human resources.(Smartsheet(2021).

Leon C. Megginson(1977), a scientist of this century, may be known and interpreted in different ways, but we can give human resources the following definition: Human resources are knowledge, skills, creativity, talent and behaviour and symptoms found in humans.

So from a general point of view they represent the sum of the innate abilities, educational knowledge and skills trained in the performance and value of the staff.

Researcher Leon C. Megginson described social capital as "social and emotional and intellectual capital" consisting of personal specializations, valuable knowledge and skills, natural cognition and the ability to learn academically and the necessary skills known as human capital.

Social capital consists of inter contacted and interconnected relationships, which are social, trust and confidence of communities. The capital of societies consists of self confidence, morale, ambition and courage, and the ability and resilience of human beings to face potential dangers.

Human resources are based on two factors: the size and quality of the workforce and the behaviour of the union in which the workers employed. Also important are learned and natural knowledge, diplomacy and professionalism, compassion and accountability to others, knowledge of work and other issues and a positive view of social aspects and justice and resilience.

In addition to improving job satisfaction, increasing productivity and business profitability, and providing employees with better training to increase their knowledge and capacity building.

The origin of HRM is a recent history but it has gone through different stages with different circumstances and names, starting with manpower, personal management, human resources and now HRM, which HR is now a competitive operating in the competitive market in which organizations and companies compete freely, and the workforce are the most important resource for any organization. Planning for the required staff took a long time, and it later turned into human resource management.

American writers Terry and Franklin (1996) developed the term 6 "M" of management including Men, Material, women Money, method and market. Manufacturing and marketing, all of which are related to product management and resource mobilization and non-productive resources created by both men and women.

A better way to understand the philosophy of HRM requires a better understanding of the theory-based changes in personal management thinking

5.4 Functions of the HRM department:

HRM functions is including planning and organizing, directing and controlling the staff to perform their jobs, and controls the activities of the outside or need work or are not moving staff, recruitment of staff, selection and employees placement of personnel and placement of movement of workers, training and implementation skills planning.

These include the work of the HRM Department in the planning and promotion of staffing, rewards and staff compensation. Designing and streamlining work schedules encouraging and evaluating work performance, reward management and boosting morale and maintenance services.

The HRM department also liaises with the labour unions and trade unions, and deals with labour union and trade union bargaining, decision-making and contractual agreement with the relevant parties ' labour unions and employers' unions. The HRM department also conducts staff registration, research and employee supervision during working hours and management of work stays and vacations.

HRM is the central management and administration of the organization and serves the various divisions of staff and senior management of the organization. The HRM Department works in the Rewards Assessment System, the Marketing of Financial Systems Division of the Human Resource Production System.

Human resource planning

Human Resource Management (HRM) helps the organization to get an accurate estimate of the number of staff required to carry out the organisation's activities.

It comments on the various vacancies in the business or within the organization to understand and plan the specific skills required for the jobs to be filled. The actual information related to filling the vacancy helps the company to fill the right person for the job.

Recruitment of staff

It helps businesses or organizations hiring people with the knowledge and skills to do the job, which stores a lot of talented information that will even be available when needed in the future. HRM selects and hires employees in accordance with company rules and regulations.

Retaining employees:

 The HRM also contributes to the retention of employees in the organization or company, which means that the employees stay in the company for a long time and do not leave immediately. It also monitors the work environment, which requires that the workplace is a clean workplace, taking care of the needs of employees such as receiving adequate compensation, and special rewards or benefits. , which creates an atmosphere of joy and excitement for the staff to do the work assigned or expected.

Enhancing the effectiveness of the organization

HRM plays an important role in increasing a company's overall productivity so that it can profitably compete in the commercial market. HRM also develops and closely monitors the planning to ensure that all company products are used efficiently and effectively. And this department works to find the right person and do the right job, which helps the organization to work efficiently and effectively.

Handles disputes and queries

The Human Resources Department is responsible for resolving all employment disputes, and resolves them. Human Resource Management works to ensure that the work of the organization or company goes smoothly, and tries to address all staff concerns and grievances in accordance with labor rules and regulations.

Employee motivation:

Human Resource Management also works to encourage and motivate employees so that they can fulfill their mission and achieve their goals. This makes that possible rewarded for their performance and provision of care facilities. It monitors and reviews their level of productivity, and determines the most appropriate way to motivate them, which enhances the overall morale of employees.

Improves employee engagement:

HRM works to create a good relationship between the management of the company and its employees in order to achieve the business goals of the company or organization. It pays salaries in a fair and equitable manner, and meets the general needs of the company's employees.

HRM works to strengthen the relationship between employer and employee by implementing and respecting their ideas and proposals for the formulation and implementation of employment-related policies.

5.5 HRM objectives:

HRM objectives are including: producing more high-quality work that is satisfying, as well as self confident, and employees should feel that the work is appropriate for their abilities and knowledge and that they are treated well and fairly. And it is true that when employees are happy with the work they automatically produce a lot of product.

HRM department is aware that there are concerns that unsatisfied staff attendance at the workplace and they most of the time are absent in the workplace and they always produce a result under the required job performance. However, it is important that employees who are satisfied and those whom are dissatisfied are treated equally, and those who are unhappy at work need to be encouraged to change their mind and be satisfied with the work they are doing so that productivity can increase.

The purpose of HRM activities is to get the job done to increase the cost of living during working hours and providing with an overview that outlines important work-related factors such as management and supervision practices.

This is the basis for employees to have the freedom and autonomy to make decisions about work, to be satisfied with the surrounding physical environment, to have a safe work environment, to work hours and to be satisfied with employees. The work environment must be orderly, and the needs of the staff must be met as much as possible in order to achieve the desired goal.

HRM's objectives are also to communicate and implement policies for senior staff throughout the organization. HRM must always abide by the policies, programs, and the procedures should be better to apply organization policies and that any action taken in accordance the polices, and to represent the organization outside, the authority of the organization is to understand is the HRM policy and what it is about and how it handles how to deal with any emerging issues.

The objectives of the HRM work include the implementation of ethical policy and social responsibility. HRM managers must be examples and role models for HRM operations to be equitable, reliable and honest. People must not be discriminated against, and these fundamental rights must be protected, and these principles must be applied to the work of HRM in all its aspects.

It is also important that HRM activities accelerate and facilitate activities within the organization and the services or business provided by the organization such as improving customer service, introducing new products and services, training technicians and managers, and to reduce decision-making time to a shorter period of time, to increase the knowledge and training of managers, to recruit and select trained and skilled people, to promote the name and reputation of the organization and greatly reduce the decision-making time and execution of the work activities of the organization or company.

5.6 Present and Current of HR situation:

The current view of human resources is aimed at three areas: identification, maintenance and human resource development.

The science and technology are growing and moving at such a fast pace, as is the world economy and business activities increased constant. And there is a international connections and so called globalization process which has resulted in global corporate competition and the demand for skilled workers in the world and the fact that large companies in rich countries(

Multilateral companies) operating in poor developing countries are causing Economic competition and HRM with small companies, which in turn led local workers in developing countries to adapt and compete with workers in larger companies who are possessed more knowledgeable and experienced compared than those residing in developing countries.

It has also been heavily influenced by global labour competition, ongoing research on HRM and how to improve it, and the availability of new skills required in the labour market.

There has also been an increase in the impact on issues related to the capacity and knowledge of the staff, and the development of new international, regional and national regulations.

Workers' health and safety concerns are also compounded by stress and depression, which can lead to mental illness and retirement from work or leave work permanently.

1.   The role of changing professionals is human and not commodity as was once believed. HRM departments must operate on an indiscriminate basis, working organizations are made up of human beings.

     People are not invisible but can be seen, heard, touched and felt. People have God-given talents and abilities that can determine the success or failure of an organization, and in order to achieve the desired success the staff must be productive and creative in line with the needs of the organization.

2.   War of talent: the most important resource for the next 20 years is expected to be talented, smart, modern entrepreneurs, highly educated people, foreign professionals who will be employed, educated young people and will be the leader of the associations, and will be the chief executive of the more professional adults.

The staff needs to constantly further develop their knowledge, experience and abilities. It is also important that the employee has a good relationship with the senior management of his or her organization.

It is also important that HRM has a virtual operating system: there are four reasons why an organization should operate online:

1. Reduce costs, and automate system upgrades

2. Focus on HRM activities, which allow HRM to develop a strategic plan without the concerns of the organization's customers.

3. To have good and effective technology, to achieve common benefits to enable the technology to be updated at all times.

4. In each of the HRM function held in the organization and there is no external called HRM.

5. Health: Employees need to balance work and life. There are no benefits for tired competitors, sick and mentally ill workers. Employers' organizations and companies recognize that there is a link between health and employee performance.

According to labour statistics by 2020, it is in second place, followed by heart disease, which causes the highest number of disabilities in the world, and is at the forefront of mental health problems that threaten labour productivity.

6. Diversity of the staff:

Employment diversity has a wide range of issues related to gender equality in terms of gender, minority / status, or 'hate'. Employee diversity is an important factor in business strategy, which can be key to solving a variety of problems and making informed decisions.

7. Technology is evolving and increasing its impact on our personal lives and those related to the workplace. Technology should tie the knot in managing the relationship between customers and employees of the organization

8. Leadership Development: Leadership requires progress and growth, and leadership skills development is not taught in schools or receiving training. Management is the work of what you do and the people you lead to do the tasks assigned to you; In order for a leader to be successful in his or her leadership plan, it is important that he or she learns the requirements and characteristics to be able to perform effectively and visibly. Leadership comes with empowerment. Employees do not become leaders until they have the ability to make decisions in the face of various risks, which in turn determine and create creativity, innovation and leadership.

8. Good governance.

The challenge for HRM professionals is to monitor the organization to reach out to talented people and people who are thinking about a brighter future. There are various companies and organizations that have made plans to find the number and staff needed to fill the professional gap in the organization or business.

9. Integration of values and culture. Good manners and ethics are important to the proper conduct of the union staff. Cultural improvement is required to comply with all established rules and policies regarding the behaviour of union staff members in group customs and practices.

10. The impact of cultural and ethical issues and cultural adherence is one that requires a thorough monitoring of all applicable laws, and organizations and their employees need to follow the established rules.

Finally, if the company and its productivity is good, but has no sector operates on a strong HRM , this can be affected the development and success of the planned political and strategy the company.

5.7 Pros and Cons HRM management:

5.7.1 Pros:

Aline Sampras(2019), First and foremost, any organization that has a staff should have a human resources management department. We recognize that HRM is the most important asset of an organization, because the HRM Department contributes to the organization's strategy, as well as managing the staff performing the key functions of the organization. Therefore, this unit needs to be empowered to carry out its mandate.

The human resources manager is one of the most important managers in the world organizations, and provides the orders and responsibilities expected of the HR manager.

1. Good growth:
Every member of the organization is aware of the importance of the human resources manager. It is well known that the HRM department is responsible for the growth and development of the organization's staff, which manages rewards and promotions, which is a testament to the fact that this department provides significant professional growth for organizations and businesses.

2. Good pay:
The department also works to pay salaries, which are based on the employee's knowledge and experience. This contributes to the growth of the profession, which as the career increases can affect the increase in wages and other rewards received by the employees. The manager and staff of the human resources department are also given more consideration and respect.

3. Management:

Human Resource Managers manage and operate the overall financial management related the employees such as wages and the payment of and rewards and bonuses or other financial rewards, and also apply labor law by applying the employer's financial requirements, which include accountability and profitability for both employer and employee.

4. Provides better management experience:
The Personnel Resources Department also works to nominate vacant candidates for the company or organization. This ensures that the new employee meets all the requirements. The department provides employees with a good knowledge of job responsibilities and responsibilities.

5. Strengthened strategic thinking:

The HRM department contributes to the development of the company's overall strategy, and the company manager must come up with ideas for the company's strategy and how to improve HRM development so that the company can be profitable and productive much to then achieve the company's goal. That is to say, to come up with ideas that can lead to development and renewal.

6. Better job satisfaction:

It is important that the HR manager is a person who knows the duties and responsibilities required, and can work with other departments to understand their responsibilities and obligations, which requires that each employee understand the value of the job to the individual responsibilities delegated.

The HR manager and other staff should be satisfied with the work assigned to them and be evaluated. This requires the general management of the company to be encourage and motivated so that the employees can do their job well.

7. Communication Skills:
It is important for HRM management to have a high level of communication skills that communicate with other union employees and union leaders which in turn helps the company to have a better relationship with the employer and the employees.

5.7.2 Disadvantages of Being a Human Resource Manager:

Each job has its pros and cons and the disadvantages of being an HR manager include the following:

1. Maintaining a safe distance:

Most staff believes that human resource managers are difficult to communicate with. That is, the department is between two fires(Employees and Employers), each of which is likely to propose a list of complaints or conditions, leading to the decision to take a healthy distance in order to remain neutral.

At the outset, the department provides staff with information and explanations about the job, duties and behavior expected of the employee. The department manager is expected to distance himself and not be too close to the staff so that he can be safe and do his job well.

2. Higher competition:

The human resources manager works to ensure that employees are satisfied with the work as outlined in the benefits that in turn create competition among employees. Increased competition among workers can then lead to problems and disruptions for workers to attack and alienate each other, and this can be achieved through negative manpower management.

The growth rate of competition itself cannot be overstated as a general benefit to an organization or company.

3. Lower recognition value:

When a person is recognized as having done a good job, he/she feels great joy and happiness. Then HRM managers are not given any rating when evaluating employees or other similar managers, which can lead to the HRM manager feeling that they are not being given the value and consideration they deserve.

5.8 International Human Resources Management Perspective

Globalization has put pressure on the HRM department to have a global orientation that pays special attention to the diaspora or business people operating overseas and the potential challenges of modernized globalization.

International Human Resources can be defined as the process of procurement, planning and utilization of human resources in relation to global trade.

This requires companies to take into account and understand the laws of the country, the requirements for foreigners working in that country such as obtaining a visa to stay in the country, a work permit, the way in which taxes are paid in that country.

Foreign workers should be aware of the culture, geography and history of the country in which they want to work.

Also, the manager of an international company operating in a foreign country should be aware of the differences between HRM domestically and IHRM, so that he can take into account the circumstances in which foreign workers may face each other in the countries around them. climate, housing, culture and language.

Absence from family and political parties and the need for special attention to the circumstances that may result in such issues, which should be given to foreigners for the first time they arrive in the country and before he arrives and prepares so that it is easier for him to adapt immediately by paying attention to the culture and customs, the gender relation, the food, the dress code, the laws that apply to foreigners in the country.

The worker also needs help with the accommodation, to translate what he or she needs to know about the new country, and what may be allowed in his or her country but may not be allowed in this country.

It should also be explained as personal taxes, housing, children's education, health care, entertainment, emergencies and alerts to potential security threats such as kidnappings, terrorism and robbery.

In recent times the world has changed and there are many companies that are very interested in expanding their business and operating in different countries around the world, which has led HRM to adapt to this.

There has been a boom in international trade, which has resulted in many companies crossing the border and becoming more global, which in turn has reduced the competition for human resources that was previously limited to local ones to international ones.

This requires workers in different countries to be prepared for the fact that in your home country foreign workers can compete in the labor market even if you live in a low-income country. To prepare for the competition and it is open to him to travel to work in other countries of the world.

You need then prepare for the competition so that the international workers can then compete internationally for the local jobs that come out or the opportunities available in different countries of the world.

This issue of globalization should also be taken into account by politicians, academics, business people and academics in order to be successful in the global labor market, which requires you to operate efficiently and effectively within the country.

The employee to prepare to become an international competitor with the requirements and characteristics required to get a job with international companies or organizations operating in the world.

In order to achieve this, it is necessary to change the mindset of the individual, the dream of the employee, and it is necessary to reform the schools and other educational institutions to prepare the young students to be competitive and able to get employment and seek a job in the world.

We can define globalization as a way of communicating, integrating globally and then developing economies, with a focus on technologies such as IT, social media, economics, politics and culture.

HRM implements and enforces labor policies and regulations in the country in which the company operates, and contributes to the development of the organization's overall strategy by focusing on the recruitment of new employees, and the training and rewards of the organization.

5.9 Summery and Conclussion

Human resource management is the process of acquiring, and recruiting the right people with the right skills and abilities to perform the required job. HRM is one of the most important tasks of the management team in the company, which helps the organization to find a skilled workforce that contributes to the success of the company, which works to develop the skills and the satisfaction of the employees, which requires that the staff themselves have their needs addressed and given the attention they need.

HRM is always important to the organization or business that works to find the right staff, selection and recruiting as well as training and development, evaluation and performance, promotion of the workforce. It also works to strengthen the relationship between the employee and the employer.

The HRM department also works with other company executives to ensure employee entrepreneurship, performance appraisals, bonus planning, rewards and promotions.

The globalization system has made it easier for the world to come together and seem to live together in a small village. Over the past two decades, there have been international agreements that have made it easier for companies to be orientated and operate globally to access international markets, with their businesses crossing specific boundaries, enabling the development of telecommunications, transportation, and infrastructure.

It has made it easier for the world to integrate and communicate, international community not only share trade, services and economy but also they share events like disasters news, happiness and sadness.

Larger companies are now trading cross the border around the world, leading to a boom in the global labor market, with local and international workers competing for most of the jobs, leading to a shortage of skilled labour his job or another to be competitive and always develop and improve his skills and knowledge.

Also, given the high level of competition in the market, and the fact that organizations and companies are struggling to reform and revise their work ethic, HRM policies must be competitive and up-to-date. Their rights are also set out in the policy and the duty of the employee to fulfill them.

The policy has to have a positive impact on the Employees, which are the organization's most valuable asset and it is important to focus on, in order to develop a policy that encourages employees to be content to work for the organization or the company in order to increase the productivity of the organisation.

HRM focuses on increasing and enhancing the company's efforts to improve the efforts and capabilities of its employees so that the organization can achieve its goals.

5.10 Recommendations:

1. Easily increase the number of skilled workers as needed.

2. The staff be cohesive composed of different sections of the society, and pay attention to the groups that do not benefit from the ongoing developments such as women with children, youth, and other disadvantage groups

3. Raise employee expectations and create motivation and morale so that they can work more efficiently and effectively.

4. Keep abreast of changes such as improvements in IT usage.

5. Increase and continuously update the knowledge and skills of the staff.

6. Workers should strive to build on their individuality so that they are ready to succeed in international labor competition.

7. Encourage employees to innovate so that they can brainstorm and come up with new production plans and designs.

8. Carry out regular surveys to determine the motivation and satisfaction of the employees of the organization or company.

9. Develop a plan with clearly defined policies and procedures outlining the rights and obligations of employees.

10. Strengthen communication between HRM management and staff and the general staff and their management to facilitate communication and understanding of the work.

11. Maintain training for staff to improve their knowledge and skills.

12. Conduct an annual review to see if the plan has been implemented and why the tasks that were not expected to take place did not materialize but were delayed.

12. Avoid telephone conversations in public places during the working hours

13. Turn down the volume during workplace conversations, so that others are not disturbed.

14. Avoild on to long conversations or move to designated meeting places

15. Show respect and esteem when walking in the office with others. Holding planned meetings in conference rooms

16. Provide staff with the ability to control their projects, but maintain project guidelines, goals, deadlines,

17. To be given the power to the staff in order to make work-related decisions so that they can work independently and take the necessary advice to make the right decisions.

5.11 References:

Deslandes G., (2014), "Management in Xenophon's Philosophy : a Retrospective Analysis", 38th Annual Research Conference, Philosophy of Management, 2014, July 14–16, Chicago

Dubrin, Andrew J. (2009). Essentials of management (8th ed.). Mason, OH: Thomson Business & Economics. ISBN 978-0-324-35389-1. OCLC 227205643.

Frank, Prabbal (2007). People Manipulation: A Positive Approach (2 ed.). New Delhi: Sterling Publishers Pvt. Ltd (published 2009). pp. 3–7. ISBN 978-81-207-4352-6. Retrieved 2015-09-05. There is a difference

Harper, Douglas. "management". Online Etymology Dictionary. Retrieved 2015-08-29. – "Meaning 'governing body' (originally of a theater) is from 1739

Investopia(2019, onlineavailable: https://www.investopedia.com/terms/o/operations-management.asp, retrieved on 25/11/2021

Gulshan, S. Management Principles and Practices by Lallan Prasad and SS Gulshan. Excel Books India. pp. 6–. ISBN 978-93-5062-099-1

John M. Ivancevich, William F. Glueck(1989), Foundations of Personnel: Human Resource Management, BPI/Irwin, 1989, Pennsylvania State University.

Dessler (2008), human resources management, Upper Saddle River, NJ : Pearson Prentice Hall.

Megginson, Leon C., Personnel and Human Resources Administration, Richard d. Irwin Inc., Homwood, Illinois.

Sametsheet 2021), Human resources management. Access https://www.smartsheet.com/human-resource-management, Retreived on 12/01/2022

Aline Sampras(2019), The Pros and cons of being HR Manager

https://www.hrmexam.com/2019/08/08/the-pros-and-cons-of-being-an-human-resources-manager.

Randstad (2019), 6 ways HRM can improve employee productivitt. Onlineavailable: https://www.randstadrisesmart.com/blog/6-ways-hr-can-improve-employee-productivity, access 01/02/2022

ChAPTER SIX

6.   What is Operational Management?

Investopia(2019) Operational management can be defined as the management of business behaviors to create the most effective and efficient production within the organization or company, and is related to the conversion of goods and other business services into more efficient and effective services, possible to then increase the company's productivity.

Operational management is the process of managing the design and control of the production process and restructuring the business operations of a product or service.

Operational management also involves the acquisition of manpower, technology, and systems within a company with the necessary experiences and capabilities related to the delivery of the organization's goods or services.

This part of the operation also manages the direct routes that are necessary for the company to produce and then access the products and services provided by the company.

The operational unit also works to learn the behaviors and skills in the designing, planning, and implementation of production systems and processes to achieve organizational goals.

Operational management is the business model responsible for planning, organizing, coordinating and controlling, maintaining the resources needed to produce the products needed by the company. It is the management of a complete production process, and streamlines and integrates production materials into the finished goods and services system.

Operational management is the management of business practices in order to create a high level of environment based on the most effective potential within the organization. Operations management is busy converting goods and services into products and services in the most appropriate way possible.

The company's operational management professionals work to balance the company's expenditures and revenues to maximize the company's net profit from operations.

Operation management manages and operates business input such as;

- Goods
- Machines
- Work
- Management
- Finance

The operation also manages the output:
- Goods
- Pollution Indirect Waste Services
- Services To Direct Production Products

Operational management also manages the internal production process and
Export: Export: Legal, Economic, Social, Technical, Labor, Capital, Consumption.

The operation department also manages the change process that exists within the company
and the existing Relationships related to product changes in standard systems.

Pardeshi, R(2020) Each company contains different parts so that it can perform its functions.
We can say that operational management is the collection of people (employees), technology,
and other relevant systems of the company.

In order for the company to achieve its business objectives, it required to have the skilled
workers to do the job well, the equipment and tools to operate, the resources and the vehicles
to be used to deliver the products that the customers need. This unit engages in and works
closely with other sectors such as sales, marketing, etc, which use planning, design,
coordination and product control to achieve the organization's goals.

This department does the most important job of designing and working on a business product
or direct product that the company is famous for.

This is the part where the necessary resources are invested in the company, such as those
mentioned above. This translates the products or services of the company into a complete and
usable product, which in turn converts the input or output required by the company into a
complete product that is ready to be marketed and sold.

It is said that production is bigger and more valuable than what is invested to get mountain
production. Every organization or company that sells its products has its own production
department (PM) or operating division. The business or service provided by these companies
depends on the size and capacity of the company, some of them are small and may be run by
one person, while there are also medium-sized companies and large companies or
organizations.

A company's production depends on the business or service capacity of the company. And there are product management and operational management that some companies have in common, while others may be different but often do the same job in both of these areas, although they may be called by different names but it is true that do the same thing in these two parts. In some companies the product is a unit or branch of the operational management department.

The operational managers have a heavy responsibility, and have a direct responsibility for the production and delivery of goods and services.

It is important that the company owns and works to ensure efficient operation so that they can benefit from market competition. The OM department is responsible for promoting the productivity and profitability of the company or organization.

Operational management or product management is related to any activity performed by an organization. In other words, every manager is an operator as he or she contributes to the creation and delivery of the operations required to perform a product or service related to an organization or company.

Some experts argue that the definition of engagement is much larger and we can specify the exact amount of product to be produced in time and quality and at a reasonable price to then satisfy customers.

As managers, participatory operations are responsible for managing the organization's product or service.

Operational managers also participate in the running and implementation of other related activities of the organization such as the marketing department; accounts; finance; staff and the Technical Department. It is important for engagement managers to make decisions:

1. Products related to product design.
2. Management operating system.
3. Improving the operating system.

 Types of operational management:The five types of decision-making each of these relate to:

1. Procedures for the production of goods and services

2. Product quality.

3. Productivity (operational capacity)

4. Inventory needed to produce goods.

5. Staff needed to be mobilized to increase productivity.

6.2 Production management:

Wiley(2009)In retrospect the history of the production management system has a long history dating back to 5000 BC. When the Sumerian government system which was developing the old system of making and producing goods, official loans for tax collection and trade etc.

The second time they had it was 4000 BC which was the time when the Egyptians started planning and building large projects such as pyramid construction.

By 1100 BC, the time of division, about 370 Xenophon explained the benefits of dividing the various necessary functions.

Participants were also involved in the division of labor, including operations and other organizational and corporate management divisions.

In the Middle Ages, the monarchy and the land regimes also developed into a system of management and operation. In those days there was a system of social hierarchy where people were divided into classes based on hierarchy and social ideology known as the Feudal system and at that time there were no strict labor laws but there were workers enslaved and workers were not paid or had no rights, they were only given food to eat and a place to sleep.

In addition to these workers, we also employed skilled craftsmen and at that time. There was connection and collobation with tradesmen and craftsmen who did the types of work that existed. Types of production methods used by manufacturers and service companies

As mentioned above production requires planning and process, which requires consultation and brainstorming in order to decide what type of product to then use to grow the business of the organization or company.

Then there is the need to develop a plan and strategy to create a better production or service system. Attention should be paid to the type of product or service that is always tailored to the appropriate marketing strategies and guidelines with regard to its goals and objectives which always keep in mind the market demand and the needs of the customers of the company or organization.

There are production methods that are generally divided into two parts:

6.3 Production Process: How do I make it?

(1) how to convert production materials into production and
(2) the time of the operation. .

6.3.1 General Product:

Large or large scale production, of which many products are produced at the same time, for example production during the industrial revolution that developed in England in the 18th century, and for example the production of industrial vehicles and the pharmaceutical industry that produces medicines and other homeopathic remedies.

The purpose behind the production of these products is to produce mass of the same products of the same name and color at the same time, the aim is to reduce costs so that prices are cheaper so that the products have a market to sell. As a result, many products enter the market at once and it becomes very difficult to buy goods at same time.

Only You: Customized Products

This type of production uses a wide range of manufacturing techniques, but the distinguishing feature of mass production is that the product or service is tailored to take into account the needs or preferences of specific customers.

This is different from mass production which is to produce more products but different in color and branding of products based on the demand and preferences of different customers of the company.
For example, a print shop project can produce or work on a variety of materials such as journals, brochures, and various magazines, print books, etc. That everything that is printed varies with the number, quality, closure, color of the line and the type of paper each company then considers and takes into account the feelings and demands of customers is called the employment shop.

Providing customized services:

There are some types of service businesses that offer specialized services, such as physicians who take into account patients' illnesses and other conditions and then pay close attention to the patient and then listen and ask questions to determine the true cause of the illness.

 The doctor may decide that he or she has a better understanding of the pain the patient is suffering from, which may lead to a diagnosis, send an extra investigation to confirm the illness, or give him a test medicine and say look at that medicine and make another appointment.

There are a number of basic ways to convert raw materials into basic products. In which natural products, human resources and machines and other combined materials can be created or converted into production.

An airplane, for example, is made up of thousands of different pieces of natural materials. Iron is brought in and then heated to convert those metal and other raw materials into metal, and then iron and other necessary materials are made in the aircraft.

6.3 Trending production management:

Shuhab-u-Tariq(2011), Since the industrial revolution that took place in the UK in 1769, the maintenance of the current changes in the management of the current product known as the Internet, investment management and production has made great strides and significant changes which have made the production of business-based services a new design.

That led to the redesign of the process of productive development and global change in relation to the world trade and economy which is the key to global development and the near and distant future of world trade.

Changes in the world that have led to rapid economic and technological development have led to constant changes in operational management related to production and commercial services.

Operations management desired to keep pace with business needs as there are new changes affecting the operational management process. The automated computing system facilitated the creation, design and operation of a product management plan, enabling computer assisted operations to design and manufacture products using operating systems, which in turn contributed to the development of new products and services. Redesigning production processes, which has resulted in saving time and money through the use of computer-based operating systems.

The transport of goods has also been modernized, which in the past was a long and time-consuming process due to the shortening of the life cycle of goods. Each product is can replace a new one in a very short time. This has made it necessary for companies to make rapid progress in developing new products with innovative products that can be replaced with new products in a very short time.

It is also important that supply chains adapt to customer needs, as product life cycles have become shorter, and there is a need to take advantage of rapid changes in product management. The use of new technologies that facilitate production, because suppliers can bring new experiences and tactics to the production team.

Managers also need to build long term partnerships and collaborations with key partners in the supply chain.

In the past, large scale production was associated with large-scale economic growth, but now there is a more flexible production that takes into account the personal preferences of the business.

Changes in the current management of operations are influenced by the productivity of the product, which is scheduled to be delivered whenever and wherever it is needed. This is due to the fact that the previous production model was designed which resulted in a new creative operation based on a good and efficient system.

In the past, service providers and businesses have also paid close attention to employees in the workplace, and it has been found that in the workplace, employees need more knowledge, experience and skills to carry out their assigned work responsibilities. In order to achieve this, staff must receive the care they need, as well as the reinforcement and training they need.

So that they can work with enthusiasm for the work we have done as part of the company. The management of the union or the company should know that the most important assets of the company are the employees of the company who need reinforcement, training, care and encouragement and how to make personal and tangible progress.

It is also important to consider the safety and well-being of the environment in which the company operates and to ensure that it does not harm the environment in which the company operates and the environment in general, because the damage is done anywhere in the world, can affect the whole world because we live on the same planet.

Therefore, the management or production department should strive to produce and benefit without harming the environment, so that the equipment and energy it consumes do not harm the environment. It is also important that the area around or near the workplace is clean and free of any wast that could harm the environment.

Operational managers are increasingly concerned about product design and sustainable ecosystems. So the design, the bags and the packaging of the various products using the resources should not be harmful to the environment, and it is better to use environmentally friendly recyclables to be reused instead of being disposed of as waste to harm the environment.

6.4 Operation management linked market competition:

Each activity is accompanied by a competition, which is contested individually and as a team. Then there is competition, especially in other businesses, to attract customers to the market.

We can define the competitive advantage of a company that sells its product or service, and delivers it to its customers in the market. This is how a company or organization finds a market for the products they are buying, which is a technique or strategy used to attract customers in the market with the same eyes as other companies to buy products that your business or company sells.

6.5 How to get the most out of market competition:

Attracting and appealing to customers is one of the most important tasks of a company, so managing the engagement department works with the marketing department to produce good quality products and services at low cost. This can be achieved by offering customers high quality, value-added products.

Then each company should think about how to understand the demands and behavior of customers, and what motivates customers to buy their product or service, how to attract businesses or companies that hold your product does not offer the same service as you have.

To understand this, a set of key purchasing criteria has been developed, including the following:

Price: Companies need to know how much the customer wants to buy the item or product they want to buy. It is important to understand that the company understands that if the product is the same different companies are selling it will turn to the cheaper product compared to other businesses.

Quality, the customer also needs to buy a quality product or product, in addition to the logo, color and brand name of the company or brand, the customer is also interested in the product he bought and paid for good quality that can be used for a long time, which does not immediately or quickly deteriorate or become defective.

Variety. Consumers also like to have a variety of products with different logos, colors, and shapes and styles available, so that they have the opportunity to choose from.

Timeliness of access to goods and services. Customers are also interested in the time they can receive a product or service when they order and most consumers would rather not buy out as much as they should have. It is important that the company delivers to its destination as soon as possible and does not have to wait for an unwanted time because the customer may need the item quickly and cannot wait too long.

6.6 Operational strategy:

Companies and businesses engaged in the production of various products and services, operate in a system that improves the use of materials, people and other related means.

It is important to make sure that the system works properly and that efforts to achieve the goals and objectives of the company are the top priorities of the existing business.

To achieve this it is important to have a strategic plan of action, which will then help you with the company's plans and other activities related to achieving the company's procedures.

The activation strategy is related to decision making after the analysis is over. Organizations and companies pay special attention to the steps to be taken in the production and delivery of the goods and services needed to be marketed.

We can say that strategy is the implementation strategy in the various production areas. The engagement strategy is rooted in the overall business strategy of the company, which helps the company achieve its overall goals and market competition for the benefit of companies.
For example, a furniture manufacturer may do the following:

- Product availability
- Working with suppliers
-Designing new furniture
- Production of furniture designs
- Personnel management
- Production of finished furniture and delivery to sellers or customers.

6.6.1 Strategy engagement answers the following questions:

What products can be produced, how much is needed, and at what facility? Couldn't the company produce all the required products, which ones are urgently needed, and which facilities are needed? Where are these centers located? How powerful are these centers? What kind of technology needs to be used and what level is required?

How the product will be distributed to the end customers. Who distributes the goods or materials, and to what extent, what skills are needed for the staff?

An operational strategy we can say is a combination of total decisions that make it easier to build long term capacity for any type of activity and work out the overall business strategy of the company through reviewing market demand and products operations. The engagement strategy is rooted in the overall business strategy of the company.

The business strategy must take into account the realities of the strengths and weaknesses of the market, and the operational strategy must work and take into account how the company's business strategy is designed and structured so that the company can work together to support the goals of the organization or business.

6.6.2 Priority competing capabilities:

 Wiley (2010) highlighted operation priorities. The Operational Strategy is the responsibility of the company to ensure that all activities performed are in the correct order, which is the

planning process for the design and management of operations. This is in line with the company's overall business strategy. Focusing on competitive priorities in the following areas:
- Price
- Quality
- Time
- Flexibility

6.6 .3 Competing on Price:

Selling products at a low price is one of the strategic priorities that a business can bring to market competition. Macaulay offers high-quality, low-cost products compared to other commercial markets. So low cost products do not automatically mean that our quality is low.

On the other hand, this needs to be balanced because cheap products to attract customers should not cause the company to lose its profits.

6.6.4 Competing on Quality

Quality is also one of the strategic qualities of selling products, quality is defined in a personal way, it is defined or interpreted in different ways, quality is related to the design of high performance of the product, along with high product specifications with durability high, excellent customer service that can be rated at a high level. Quality also includes sustainability and access to goods and services. The products are carefully crafted and carefully selected when marketed, which means that there are no defects or errors. Most companies have a unit called quality controle that works and checks the quality of the product. This is a pre-requisite for products and services that ensure that the company produces quality products that are flawless and flawless.

6.7.5 Competing on time:

Time or speed to design, manufacture and complete a product is one of the most important strategies for a business or service provider. When it takes time for a product to arrive rather than be bought or marketed it is very important for both traders and consumers.

It is best to shorten and lengthen the process between ordering goods and services and delivery time. It is a good idea to have products available at the right time at the right time, which can help the business compete in the market.

6.6.6 Competing on flexibility:

There are many changes to the environment in which the company operates, and companies must take this into account and have developed a strategic plan to adapt to these changes.

This requires that the product be modified in a small way, and it is also important that you plan and customize the product so that you meet the specific requirements, specific features of customer orders and easily. can change.

These include competitiveness in volume, capacity to increase productivity or, if necessary, productivity reduction if demand is lower than expected, which is always important to keep production in line with market demand in order to be successful marketing goals.

6.7 Advantage and disadvantage operational management:

Planet together,(2020**)** As mentioned above operations management is the process of planning, organizing, and controlling the overall production process. The system was originally designed to address the collaborative approach of the various departments of the organization or company. So this operational management department mainly deals with production and delivery, and operational centers use a variety of methods to ensure that the planned production of the company is managed in the best possible way possible to deliver these products or delivered at the right time.

The operation department works closely with other sectors such as supply chains and logistics. Operational management works to ensure that resources are used efficiently, which significantly reduces waste, implements decisive and effective decision-making tactics, as well as reduces costs.

It is important that as project management is necessary it is also important to analyze the pros and cons of productive operations for businesses and organizations.

6.7.1 Operations Management Benefits

As mentioned above, each company needs to have its own operations department or production facility. The benefit is to increase productivity and enable the company to achieve its business goals. Operations management benefits include:

Operations management: It makes it easier for the company to better manage its production and make the company more profitable. It also makes it easier for company executives to understand and monitor the company's production and revenue. They receive important information so that important decisions can be made regarding productivity and sales growth. This makes it easier to come up with new ideas for a product or service.

- Good resource management It is important to manage all resources well and responsibly so that the business can grow and prosper. These include machines, IT systems, and other essential equipment.

- Competitive Advantage: Coordination and coordination required by the various departments of the organization or company so that the activities go smoothly as intended. It is also important that the time you spend producing the product is very short and minimal.

This allows you to deliver the goods to the market on time and without delay. This in turn strengthens the relationship between the company and its customers so that you can maximize your business profitability and win over other competitors in the market.

6.7.2 Operations Management Disadvantages

Whatever the case may be, it is important to take into account the following:
- Dependence on Different Levels: One of the disadvantages is that the various components of the company do not work properly and their communication is interrupted, even if there is a good and effective plan. This lack of cooperation will affect the company's productivity which could lead to unintended decline.

- Human error: There is a tendency for humans to make unintentional mistakes, especially during the operation. These errors often occur during production and sales. Production such as operations, marketing, finance, accounting, engineering, information, and human resources should be closely monitored and controlled.

6.8 Conclusion: How to improve operation management

Sweet process(2021) Operational management needs to be developed and updated, which requires understanding and planning, so that the organization or company is successful in its business operations.

In order to achieve the desired progress it is important to have an understanding of the strategic nature of the operation, which plays an important role in the impact of technology on the performance and success of market competition, which requires that you Understand and study the factors influencing customer behavior that make them decide and buy the products or services your business or company owns.

This focuses on the most important factors such as price, quality, characteristics and performance characteristics, product diversity, how fast the product is available, and other factors that may influence the buyer's decision.

It is also important that there is a balance between products and market demand, and that products should not exceed market demand. For example, when production increases, the price of goods or services decreases.

Operations development also includes the upgrading of production equipment, and the training and retraining of staff to be the focus of the company in the overall business strategy of the company and not only the operational management of the company.

Each company is evaluated not by cost reduction but the best international standard is: product availability, product price, quality and unique characteristics of the product, performance and product diversity.

6.9 Recommendations:

Honeywell(2019), highlighted key steps to improve operation management, which are including:

1. Know your operation: It is important that operational managers regularly monitor and evaluate the progress of the operation and the priorities of the management department such as monitoring the transport of equipment and personnel needed to carry out the operation, so that it can be maintained on a regular basis, monitors official audits, measurement comments and monitors business intelligence tools all of which are beneficial for business operations.

2. Ongoing training: It is also important to have the necessary and sustained training is important for the efficiency and effectiveness of the work provided to staff and operational management. Completion of SOP documentation, and providing supervision and couching of staff are key issues in the development of operational management.

3. Put people first: In order to encourage and motivate the staff they should get the training they need so that they can improve and stay with you and not be left behind by the staff.

Always keep in mind that people are the most important asset of an organization, so it is good to improve the relationship between employees and the company. Employees should receive a reward commensurate with the work they do, as well as rewarding the best employees, as well as discouraging unhealthy habits and practices.

4. Keep an order fulfillment focus: to increase productivity in response to customer demands, donate the right equipment to the operating department to address potential challenges, from start to finish, and be ready for needed repairs to create an environment that helps you achieve the desired business engagement goal.

5. Improving customer service. It is important to make your business based on customer service, because customers are the ones who you are focused or buy the goods and

services of the business, a strong relationship with them and their satisfaction is necessary for the process to continue.

Then products based on customer preferences, minimizing technical defects and errors, products that arrive quickly or on time are important to improve the customer relationship of the company.

6.   Remove barriers to success: Develop a plan analysis process to identify potential barriers to your business success. Be open minded and able to deal with obstacles and solutions and adapt to future changes.

6.10 Biography:

Investopia(2019, onlineavailable: https://www.investopedia.com/terms/o/operations-management.asp, retrieved on 25/11/2021

Gulshan, S. *Management Principles and Practices by Lallan Prasad and SS Gulshan*. *Excel Books India. pp. 6–.* ISBN 978-93-5062-099-1

Honeywell(2019), 10 steps improve operational management. Online available: https://sps.honeywell.com/us/en/support/blog/automation/10-steps-improve-operational-efficiency. Retreived on 05/01/2022.

Sweet process(2021),operational management online available: **https://www.sweetprocess.com/operations-management/#ch5**. **Retrieved on 10/01/2021)**

Pardeshi,R(2020), **https://www.slideshare.net/rameshsinghpardeshi/operation-management-32601309**

(Planet together, 2020)https://www.planettogether.com/blog/advantages-and-disadvantages-of-operations-management.Retrieved on 12/12/2020).

Shuhab-u-Tariq(2011), Recent Trends in Modern Operations Management, **https://www.slideshare.net/shuhabtrq/recent-trends-in-modern-operations-management**

Wiley(2010). Operations Strategy and Competitiveness, available on: https/www/csus.edu, retrieved on 06/01/2021.

Friedrick Klemm, A history of Western Technology, Charles Scribner's Sons 1959 in D. A. Wren and A. G. Bedeian, The Evolution of Management Thought, Wiley 2009.

Chapter Seven:

7. Financial management

Finance can be defined as managing, creating and analyzing money and investments. It focuses on finding answers to questions related to how a person, company or government makes money, which we know as capital in terms of business, and how that money is used or invested. (Hyes, 2021)

Finance has different components such as: private finance, corporate finance and public finance. Finance in general is initially divided into two types: public finance and private finance. Public finance is further divided into three categories:

- Central government
- Regional government
- Local governments.

Private finance falls into three categories:
- Individual finance
- Partnership finance.
-Business finance.

So in this book I am focusing on is Business finance. Business Finance management consists of three distinct components:

1. Financial management
2. Capital markets
3. Funding

7.1 Financial management in business

Financial management is related to how the business of the company works, and it is the glue that connects the business of the company, and it is also the oil that drives the machine and makes it work in a series.

Also most of the business operates and uses economic concepts and practices related to supply, demand, pricing, market segmentation, business competition and some of the other business principles we have discussed in other chapters of this book.

Financial is also related to other accounting principles and procedures, and you need to have the knowledge and skills to be able to collect, abbreviate, and analyze financial data.

Investing is also about ensuring that money flows easily and securely through the business, which can then be achieved by strengthening investments and deploying other financial resources.

Finance, therefore, refers to the study of securities. Securities are financial instruments that can be purchased and used to accumulate capital in public and private markets.

Other important financial factors include a Derivative is an agreement between two or more securities based on agreed-upon financial assets (such as collateral).

Business Finance consists of three distinct components:

1. Financial management
2. Capital markets
3. Funding

7.2 Financial management Concept

Finance is the flow of cash between the capital markets and the operations of a company. Financial management is about managing short-term financial management, which then oversees and oversees current assets and current debt.

Financial Management also focuses on managing exchange rate fluctuations and commodity cycles. They also work to manage the day to date activity of the company's finances.

Financial management also works on the long-term financial management strategy of the company, which then focuses on the long term management of the company's capital system which includes boosting the company's capital, the company's budget (asset distribution) between business units or commodities) and the company's shareholding system.

Finance then has its domain of private money management and public asset management and public finances. Finance includes tribal guarantees, financial endeavors, investment banks and financial professionals and managing risks associated with investing and spending money.

The basis of institutions and financial instruments is the valuation of assets such as shares, bonds, loans and, among other things, extensions.

There is also the fact that some people confuse finance with economics. What we can define the economy is the production, distribution and use of social goods and services, which must be financed.

While finance is investment and its tool such as accounting skills, financial accounting is the reporting of historical financial information moving forward.

7.2.1 Specific activities:

Increased profits: occurs when low costs are the same as low incomes are equal and not unequal. This is the main goal of Financial Management.

Accurate cash flow monitoring: It is important to spend on daily activities such as; raw materials, energy costs, wages, rent etc. Having enough cash for your business improves the company's growth and development and management predicts that cash flow.

Reducing capital expenditures: in financial management contributes to operations to generate more profit term is used for short term purposes related to financial manageable profits.

Estimation of Requirements Investment: Entrepreneurs further anticipate and plan for the funds required to be used by the company in the short and long term, which in turn can help improve investment.

Capital Structure Determination: The structure is about how a company invests in its overall business operations and the revenue growth of the company using different sources of revenue.

In order to achieve this, a budget requirement is made. It is important for the financial manager to determine the combination of debt and balances as well as the types of debt owed to the company.

7.3 Objectives of Finance management:

 (Paramasivan, 2010), Effective procurement and efficient use of resources can lead to better good practice. It is the main task of the financial managers of various companies. The job of a business leader is to determine the necessary or fundamental objectives of the company's financial management. The main objectives of financial management are the following:

1. Increase Profits
2. Increase in assets.

The overarching goal of all forms of economic activity is to achieve profitability and run an economic valuable business, promote effective benifit.

1. An increase in profit is also known as an increase in the cash per share of the company. It leads to increased business efficiency to increase productivity and profitability.

2. The ultimate goal of business fear is to make a profit, which is why it considers all possible ways to increase profitability.

Goals

3. Profit is the measure of the effectiveness of entrepreneurial anxiety. It then shows all place of business importance.

4. Profit-increasing objectives help reduce business risk. The best profit increase debate

The following key points support a corporate group's profitability goals:

(i) The main goal is to make a lot of money.

(ii) Profit is the purpose of the business.

(iii) Profitability reduces the risk of business anxiety.

(iv) Profit is the main source of income for a business.

(v) Benefiting also meets the needs of the community.

7.4 Capital Markets:

Hyes, A(2001) Capital markets can be defined as financial markets that connect and bring together buyers and sellers to trade stocks, bonds, currencies and other financial assets. Capital markets also include stock markets and bonds. They help visionary people to become successful entrepreneurs and help small businesses grow and become big companies in the future.

Capital markets are places where deposits and investments are made by suppliers - people or factories with capital to borrow or invest and the people who need that investment.

Distributors are typically banks and investors, while capitalists are corporations, governments, and high net worth individuals. Capital markets consist of lower and higher markets. The most popular capital markets are the stock market and the bond market.

Capital markets work to improve the efficiency of transactions. These markets bring together suppliers and capitalists and provide them with a place to find and exchange securities to encourage investment.

Capital markets are divided between suppliers and consumers. Distributors include households - which use bank accounts - as well as other investment vehicles such as pension insurers, life insurance companies, charities and not-for-pr ofit financial institutions, which generate additional money.

"Consumers" of funds invested in capital markets invested in the real estate market, auto companies and governments working to finance infrastructure and operating costs.

Capital markets are used to sell financial products such as stocks and mortgages. Shares are shareholders, which are own shares of a company. Debt securities, such as bonds, are of interest to others.

These markets come in two different categories: primary markets - where new stocks and securities issues are sold to investors, and higher markets, which trade on existing bonds. Capital markets are an important part of a functioning modern economy because they move money from holders to those who need profitable profits.

7.4.1 Funding:

With capital investments, and loans and all kinds of financing or financial assistance needed, the basis of the word funding is the basic investment needed whether it is a loan or a grant.

Fund is the acquisition of financial resources to meet a need or to carry out a program or project to be carried out where it is needed. It can also be donated in the form of an association or company.

This method is usually used when the company uses its internal reserves to meet the cash flow required to perform a dizzying task. Financing can be done from a variety of sources, including loans, business capital, grants, savings and taxes. Investments such as grants, grants that are not subject to a direct return on investment, are described as soft investments or fundraisers.

Funding meaning
Repetition,
Coincidence
Support
Innovation

7.5 Financial management and its functions:
Harappa education (2021) Financial management functions are essential to procurement finance, resource planning and use of corporate resources, among others. This is usually the responsibility of the financial managers of the company or organization. Let's focus on the role of financial managers.

1. Decisions and Control

Financial managers work and are responsible for the company or organization to advise and make decisions on fundamental issues that require financial decisions and to check and control the company's finances.

Using a variety of methods and techniques such as the company's financial forecast for the future, stock discussions and estimating profit and loss forecasts for the company, the aim is for the company to prepare for the financial risks that the company might face.

2. Financial Planning
Financial management also determines the financial planning of a company and its sources of revenue.

Managers use existing financial information to develop a plan to measure the organization's priorities and current or potential financial needs. They also focus on the overall financial situation of the Union to prepare a budget plan, so that they can make the desired decisions regarding the Union's finances.

3. Resource Allocation

Managers are also responsible for ensuring that all of the company's financial resources are used in the most efficient and effective ways. Managers oversee and constantly check whether businesses are investing effectively and efficiently. Properly planned finances lead to long-term benefits.

4. Cash flow management

Managers are responsible for controlling the organization's money or cash equivalents. Managers are able to ensure that organizations are able to cover the funding required for operational times and emergencies.

5. Disposal of Shares

Financial managers are forced to make decisions regarding the net profitability of the organisation's market share. This helps with financial objectives related to the market share that is being used or maintained.

What are the Types of Financial Management Decisions? Financial managers are responsible for making accurate predictions, and for making financial decisions.

7.5.1 Investment Decisions

Financial managers are expected to determine the amount of investment funds that are available financially, taking into account the needs of the company or organization in the near or distant future. The decisions that managers make in the long run are called capital calculations, in which companies or organizations promise long-term investments (e.g., fixed assets).

While short term investment decisions are also known as labor capital management, which requires businesses to commit to short-term investments. These include decisions regarding the financing of goods, banks and others.

2. Investment Decisions

The financial decisions that the company managers are required to make the right decision relate to the amount of money that will be collected from various sources, which can be a long term source. They need to make sure they get the funding they need. In addition, they make sure that the money is available at the right time.

3. Divided decisions.

These so called split decisions are related to checking and planning how much should be kept and not used. This is when dividends are distributed to shareholders of a company called dividends.

This is when the balance is made and deposits are made so that they can be used in the future. Making such decisions requires a thorough knowledge and deep thinking from many angles.

7.6 Advantage and disadvantage of financial management

7.6.1 Advantages:

Making good decisions about financial management makes it easier to make the right decisions at the right time.

Financial management collects and archives when all the financial information of the organization is needed, and helps the company managers to get the real facts related to the required financial conference accounts. Commercemates(2021

It is important for business professionals to keep a record of all available financial management information when it comes to accurate and effective business information. As a result, there is transparency and accountability.

Financial control
Financial management controls the organization's finances and expenditures, as well as monitors all business activities of the company to control its finances. The financial manager ensures that all business activities of the company then reflect the plans and expenses set, and

control that they are implemented and not exceed the planned budget within the company strategy.

Strengthens administrative transparency

The financial management company is responsible for maintaining the financial ethics of the company within the organization, pays close attention to the fact that the company's finances are used and discharged in a legal manner that is then beneficial and strengthens the business interests of the company. .

The finances also look at how employees in different departments can produce better and more profitable products for the company. And financial managers are always focused on increasing productivity to make more profit and also prevent the company from incurring unnecessary expenses that can be detrimental to the organization or business of the company.

Avoids Debts:

It is also important to be aware the value of money and make wisely using of the company's resources such as skilled workers, equipment, transportation and company supplies.

Financial management helps the company to be careful not to take on unnecessary debt. This in turn encourages the efficient and efficient use of all company assets, which in turn reduces the overall costs of the company, and seeks to prevent the company from taking on unnecessary debt and remaining difficult to be repaid.

Financial Management Disadvantages

Expensive

Financial management is an important issue for both commercial and non-profit organizations, and it is important to ensure that a good plan is put in place to control the spending of organizations, which takes time and resources, both manpower and equipment or materials used.

Rigidly and complexity

Financial management brings bureaucratic and complexity system as there is systems for measuring organizational performance and how much actual costs are required to be used. Guidelines and financial procedures are then designed to perform various tasks that require the use of expenditures, with different procedures and requirements, which can result in differences between previous predictions and actual figures when it comes to capture or execution that task.

Also the cost management department is doing a good job for business organizations that the financial and other expenditures used are required, but this should not cause delaying the important decisions or the company cannot make the specific commitment because of its rigidity and non-compliance unwavering commitment by financial spending guidelines.

7.7 International financial management

(Wikipedia, 2020), Business globalization refers to companies operating outside the borders of their home countries trading in foreign countries or internationally in the aftermath of World War II. This has a profound effect on the world economy and financial management leading to changes in the existing financial management system.

Countries around the world exchange goods and services for other purposes, and in terms of international trade the three most important issues related this topic are including imports, exports and the trading space available for various goods are important.

There is a world of openness and big international companies have made it easier for businesses to be global. Although in the case of international financial management automatically then it is possible to think that money trading can be done through finance through the exchange rate of currencies in different countries.

In countries around the world, foreign currency is used in order to buy and sell, as each country uses its own currency, while other countries or currencies use foreign currencies such as the dollar and the euro.

And international business ventures enable businesses to communicate and interact with customers and global suppliers around the world.

Such transactions are also used by government agencies and non governmental organizations such as charities.

At the end of World War II the GATT was formed, which was then aimed at promoting trade, and free trade was encouraged to open up the world in order to enable unlimited trade, which in turn led to international trade rises.

The Second World War also saw the emergence of international financial institutions such as the World Bank and the International Monetary Fund (IMF).

Trade relations between the two countries have increased, with many countries launching open trade liberalization policies, in which various countries have signed trade and investment agreements, Which required international financial management.

As business has become more global and unlimited, there are international companies that are taking advantage of it, especially the so called multinational companies.

As a result, financial management is functioning differently from the traditional business model and a mixed financial market, as well as a variety of international investments, is needed to achieve this or for sale.

It is also important when dealing with the global financial management of the unstable exchange rate of the world that it fluctuates and the potential health, economic and political risks to be considered when making an international investment risk assessment.

According to Uddin, there are many international companies operating around the world, and there are about 60,000 Multi National companies operating in the global market. We can say that Multi National Company is a company that operates or produces in one or more countries as well as doing business or has business centers in other countries of the world.

Some international companies are affiliated with other countries, such as importing goods from another country, they may also receive financial capital from a bank in another country, and import or produce products made with equipment. produced by another country and the capital of a third country, and the products are exported to other countries controlled by other nations. Uddin, M (2014).

If international companies are going to take advantage of the huge economy they should be able to enter and invest in global markets where there are business opportunities. But it is important that companies' entry into the international market is unique and that domestic investment in their countries of origin must be approached carefully, especially at the outset, taking into account the policies of foreign-funded investors. Economic aspect of foreign investment, and other security and political risks in those countries.

It is also important for companies to know that remittances to different countries have been tightened since 9/11. By preventing remittances from individuals or organizations suspected of supporting terrorist or other extremist organizations.

This means that all remittances go through a system that ensures that the recipients and senders of the information have access to their information in accordance with the 'know your customer' policy.

It has also tightened the exchange system in third countries, especially the Muslim ones, where most of the money goes through US banks and it takes a long time for the money to reach its destination.

This can lead to delays and disruptions in business activities and the flow of goods.

7.7.1 The importance of global financial management

There is a big difference between domestic and international financial markets, so that international markets have different perspectives, forecasts, and analysis and economic practices, so it is important that business managers know and have a long-standing professional background in managing international financial management, which in turn allows the business community to achieve greater transparency and profitability.

International companies are encouraged to do their part by doing the following:
• To export their products, so that they become cheaper and do not require logistics cost and avoiding higher import taxes.
• The raw materials necessary for the company's production are easily available in foreign countries.
• Companies have the opportunity to deliver and sell their products in a variety of markets.
• Properly managed foreign trade can result in increased revenue and foreign investment

7.8 Recommendation how to improve financial management:

Every business, whether local or international, needs good and effective financial management, which is essential for the growth and development of the business, and to avoid the risks it faces business meetings that we discussed earlier.

When we speak of financial management of a company we mean planning, organizing, controlling and monitoring the financial resources of the company.

Effective financial management helps businesses make better and more efficient use of company resources, meet and fulfill the promises of their clients and other stakeholders, and reap greater benefits from market competition. long-term financial stability. Nibusinessinfo(2021)

In order to achieve this, the following tips need to be considered.

1. The company should have a clear business plan

The business plan will guide you to where you are and where you want to be in the future. This business plan tells you how you will invest in your business and other related activities, the investments you will need and where the money will come from.

2. Monitor your finances

It is also important that the investment manager regularly monitors the activity and business development that exists. It is a good idea to keep an eye on the amount of money in the bank, the sales being made and the stock market status on a daily basis. It is also a good idea to regularly review your business plans and strategies. Also check the existing cash flow management on a monthly basis.

3. Make sure customers pay you on time

Businesses could face unforeseen financial difficulties, because customer payments can be delayed, and to prevent this you need to be clear about the terms and conditions of the loan from the very beginning, and it is important to pay off the debt as soon as possible clear and accurate claim. The company has a debt management system that allows you to keep track of your outstanding debt. Encourage customers to pay on time and without delay.

4. Know daily expenses
Companies can run into financial difficulties if they do not have enough cash to cover the company's ongoing expenses such as rent and wages.

You need to be aware of the amount of money you can spend to meet the needs and expenses of the company.

Keep up-to-date accounting records

The company's cash accounts need to be updated, otherwise the company's business is at risk of losing money, if you do not follow up regularly and make sure customers pay their debts quickly. It is a good idea to use a good system to use the expenses, loans, investments, savings or cash deposits you have.

6. Meet the tax deadline.

It is also a good idea to be aware of the deadline for filing and paying taxes, which can result in interest and fines, and these costs, can be avoided if the company arrives.

7. Be extremely capable of controlling excess
It is also important that you run your business efficiently, and that you also save energy, use equipment and other resources that you need to be aware of and take into account. The purpose is to reduce and control the costs incurred by the company.

8. Storage control

It is also important to make sure that you have the right amount of savings available at the right time so that your capital is not tied to a complex and unnecessary structure, and it is also important to keep track of stock levels.

7.9 References:

Paramasivan,C(2009), Financial management, New age international publisher, New Delhi

Hyes, A(2001) https://www.investopedia.com/terms/c/capitalmarkets.asp

Hyes (2021) Finance management, online available:
https://www.investopedia.com/terms/f/finance.asp

Uddin, M (2014) https://www.slideshare.net/mohanuddin/introduction-to-international-finance-31549903.

Wikepedia(2020), International financial resources: available online:
https://en.wikipedia.org/wiki/International_financial_management, Retreived 20/02/2022

Commercemates(2021), advantages and disadvantages of financial management, online available: https://commercemates.com/advantages-and-disadvantages-of-financial-management.

Nibusinessinfo) 2020) improve your financial management: online available:
https://www.nibusinessinfo.co.uk/content/ten-top-tips-improve-your-financial-management

Harappa education (2021) what is the financial management and its functions. Online available:
https://harappa.education/harappa-diaries/what-is-financial-managment-and-its-functions/

CHAPTER EIGHT

8. Business policy and strategy:

8.1 Introduction:

I believe that every organization, whether commercial or non-commercial, needs to have a good business policy and strategy.

The company's business policy and strategy is a system of study; linked the duties and general management responsibilities of the companies; corporate policy and strategy; and a vision that predicts the business development of a company.

 The collaboration and understanding of corporate employees and senior management; improving the connectivity of companies /organizations and the environment in which they operate; developing a basic business plan for a business company; policy vision, decision making process, business objectives, performance, requirements, structure and management characteristics.

In addition Identifying and enforcing the accounting system and profitable reports from the business and other accounting data; recognizing assessing opportunities and threats, acknowledging the strengths and weaknesses of a company, prepare to reinforce the strength, identifying the weakness and learning to develop it. Take advantage of the existing opportunities and taking protective measures to face the challenges.

8.2 Objectives for Business policy and strategy course:

- To develop strategic knowledge internationally so that the student can adapt and apply it to the real world.
- Acquire knowledge and strategies tailored to work, tools and language terminology to enable the student to identify key issues related to knowledge and skills, existing or potential business opportunities.
- Prioritizing business situation and issues and business challenges that arise to analyze and find the appropriate solution to compile decisions that affect future development and formulate implementation plans.
- To encourage the development of business skills and effective ideas for effective analysis of ideas, encouragement of implementation and governance.
- To bridge the gap between theory and practice by developing an understanding of why, when and how ideas are used and how they align and integrate real world experience to make effective business decisions and lead to a business success.
- Predicting organizational performance and success .Gaining insight into the factors necessary to be successful.
- Explain continued successes of organizations based on the theory often does not depend on the product, but on underlying competencies that enable some organizations to be continuously successful and innovative.
- To explain the performance of organizations.
- Why is one company more successful than another in the same circumstances? Relates to underlying competencies and competitors.

An organization does not have a guiding strategy; it is like a ship sailing in the ocean without a steering wheel. Ross,J and Kami, M(2016) "Without a strategy the organization is like a ship without a rudder going around in circles".

Definition:

Business Policy:

Definition:

Business policy is a measure of the level at which a company can make decisions about its subordinates, and provides an opportunity for investors and subordinates to find solutions to problems and related issues decision making without consulting the senior management of the company. MSG Content Team (2020).

Business policy is a guideline so that an organization or company can manage its actions. It defines the level at which an effective decision must be made and also takes into account the availability of the necessary resources in order to achieve the desired goal.

Business policy is a study that defines high levels of responsibility in the management of issues that need to be prioritized that can have a positive impact on the success of an organization and long-term planning.

Cukashmir (2020) Business Policy provides goal to managers to make appropriate business decisions at that time. Policy is a task that needs to be done without a set deadline. Business policy is guided by continuous action based tasks.

When making policy decisions about a business or company, others can be held accountable for their actions in a free and independent manner. Rules are the general legislation that an organization or group of people or a society as a whole understands and accepts to be practiced and used as a reference when it comes to disagreements or differences of opinion.Policy is also about how decisions are made that affect the business of the company.

Strategic management
Strategic management determines the long term safety and survival of a company. A strategy is a specific plan designed for specific plans that must be implemented in a specific time frame. A strategy is a new concept of implementing a pre planned but not yet implemented policy that defines what to do, how to do it, where to do it and when to do it according to the policy and objectives of the organization or partnership business.

Policy implementation or enforcement of the decision in order to improve or change shape to form a specific task is to be implemented in order to protect the commercial interests of company, executive decisions often need to be careful and cautious. In order to implement the strategy, each individual and group must play their part.

Strategy involves making choices or options clearly related to how to compete and who and how to run it to achieve the required success. (Welch,2019), "Strategy means making clear-cut choices about how to compete."

There are only two benefits to competing: the ability to learn from customers as quickly as possible and the ability to turn the lessons learned into action faster than the competition.

The strategy worries about the urgency and uncertainty of considering the risk factors and competitive conditions to overcome the organization or business that may have affected the operation and development of the company.

Strategies are developed in a way that reflects the needs of the company, and is based on using all available resources to protect the interests of the business.

The strategic decisions of the company are those that define all the resources and people who run the company in the area where the company operates and the communication and interaction between the two parties.

These decisions are about owning new resources, creating new ones or redistributing other plans and undisclosed secret decisions and are related to balancing the resources of organizations with threats and opportunities.

Private decisions apply to a wide range of changes as the organization operates at intermittent and ever changing stages. Improper plan or strategy can lead to wrong decisions that can lead to chaos and instability. MSG Content Team (2020)

8.3 General Analysis about the Business policy and strategy"

Types of Business Policy:

Juneja(2015) A successful business policy must have a clear set of criteria, including the following:

1. Specific: Trade policy must be specific and certain, otherwise it will be difficult to implement and achieve success.

2. Clear: Policy should be clear and unambiguous. It should be free from criticism and look at the vocabulary to understand the intended purpose. There should be no conflict and confusion when it comes to policy.

3. Reality / Trust: The policy should reflect the reality of the company, as well as a series of equations that run smoothly so that everyone can monitor and understand its performance.

4. Appropriate: The policy should be appropriate and reflect the organization's current goals.

5. Simple: The policy of the company should be simple and written in a language that is understandable and easily understood by all the members of the association.

6. Inclusive :The policy must be inclusive and non discriminatory, and should be comprehensive and not excluded any one or any group.

7. Facilitation : The policy should be easy and not difficult to understand and practice it, and should be easy to use. The policy should be simple and appropriate to do the job and do not require interpretation and should always be modified to make ongoing continues to perform tasks.

8. Stability: The policy is to create a secure and stable environment in which work is carried out, so as not to lead to chaos and confusion or to create a situation of constant conflict that may hinder its work.

NLFI(2016) A policy plan provides an overview of how an organization conducts its work to achieve its goals. In terms of financial identification, a brief policy plan is sufficient. Depending on the size of your organization, social recognition requires a wide variety.

In general, you describe the policy plans for the coming year, review them briefly and, if necessary, supplement a multi-year plan. You should therefore update and republish your policy plans each year. On the following pages you will find a list of subjects that should in any case be included in a larger or smaller policy plan.

Arrow(1971) Strategies are a set of business policy objectives and key plans to achieve those goals, described in the process of defining the business the company is in or intends to enter in relation to the type of company and its business.

The strategy put out a value organization advocates. What did the organization desires to achieve, how it wants to reach this and what is necessary to achieve this goal (people and resources).

You indicate that the focus of the organization in the coming years is emerging. What are the plans for the coming years? Policy is therefore understood to mean indicating the directions and the means by which the organization wants to achieve its objectives within the setting period.

Organization and shape these developments a threat or an opportunity for the organization (SWOT analysis). Term of a policy plan Most organizations write a policy plan for the next 3 years. Here the objective is translated into work goals. Smaller organizations usually suffice with a short-term policy plan of one year. This means that a plan / work plan is drawn up with an annual budget.

The activities for the coming year are described in a simple manner. Mission, vision and strategy In its mission, the organization defines its reason to be, its values and identity, while the vision, a glimpse of the future, describes the desired situation in the long term. The strategy clarifies how the future picture described in the vision will be achieved.

You can start with the emergence of the organization. What motivated you to set up this organization? What motivation, what change do you want to bring about with your organization or do you want to make a difference? To set up this organization. In the mission statement you actually describe what the organization stands for, where do they go for it.

Das(2017) The word "strategy" is derived from the Greek word "stratçgos"; stratus (meaning army) and "ago" (meaning leadership / movement).

This shows that many aspects of management science are derived from military or military education and that there are still many similarities.

I can say that Strategy is the action taken by managers to achieve one or more of the goals and objectives that the organization or company desires to achieve. A strategy is the path or plan that an organization or company sets out to achieve a specific goal that is to be achieved in the next period, which is part of the overall strategic plan decided by a company or organization.

An organizational strategy is the sum of all the activities of utilizing and planning the resources available, especially the environment in which the organization operates, in order to achieve the existing objectives.

It is advisable to conduct an assessment before making a formal strategy for the company in order to make the appropriate decision on the strategy of the organization or company, in consultation with the shareholders of the organization or company, customers, managers, owners, stakeholders and even your other competing and trading partners by dealing with them carefully. The strategy also sets out the reactions from organizations or companies that are competing with you or your regular partners.

Strategy we can also say is the knowledge of the objectives of an organization or company or the uncertainty of events that may arise from an organization's strategy and the need to respect the potential of others with other cultures.

Strategy is the design that encompasses an organization's decisions that outline its goals and objectives, encapsulates and summarizes key policies, plans to achieve that goal, and illuminates the type of business or service that the organization should undertake. The type of human organization it wants to be, it's activities, its finances and the contribution it plans to make to shareholders, customers and the community at large.

8.4 Features of Strategies:

1. In the case of organizations and businesses, strategy is important because it enables to predict the near future, and in order to do so, there must be a long term vision, and companies must develop a plan to deal with unforeseen events, uncertain about the business environment and how it works.

2. The strategy contributes to the future of long term development, and is not directed at or related to the normal operations of the organization or company, it is concerned with the possibility of new innovations or new products, new services, or new markets developed and the goal will be set in the near future.

3. Strategies are incorporated to take into account the reasonable behavior of customers and competitors. Employee management strategies will also pay attention to the behavior of employees.

Strategy is a well-presented design of an organization. It discusses the purpose and goal and direction of an organization or company. The strategic objective of an organization or company is to strengthen the business and strategic potential of an organization and to reduce the potential of other organizations competing with the organization.

The bottom line is that the strategy fills in the gaps between where the company is and where it wants to move and reach the goal.

8.5 How business policy and strategy topic applies to reality.

A business strategy is the process by which an organization or company puts its business map in order to reach and achieve the development and goals planned for the near future. It can easily be described as a long term business plan. Most business strategies are designed to guide the company or organization for about 3-5 years (and some companies plan for longer).

A business strategy is a guiding principle when it comes to planning long term business or service development or organization, reflecting the needs of an organization or company, which in consultation is taken as a decision, then the strategy relates to how the middle managers, in particular those directly involved, decide on the resources, who will carry out the task and when it will be carried out.

So strategy is the way in which the people who work or own an organization make the decision to work in the future in order to achieve important goals.

An effective strategy provides a clear to lead the guiding principles of the company which are the policies and rules of the organization and then outlines the steps to be taken by the company, what should be prioritized and what should not be prioritized for that specific time of year to achieve the goals of the organization or company.

The organization or company always needs to be held accountable for the customer's relationship with the company, and it is important to show the customer a service and behavior that satisfies them so that they do not leave the company or organization, and the company also must strive to find new customers so that both organization and its business can grow.

In order to put this in to practice, is required to plan and make strategy guide to reach this goal, which you want to attract and show you precisely and honestly serve to satisfied customers.

To achieve the destired a results you need to make monitoring system and to strengthen the relationship between you and your customer, and that is the form of certain customers to present their point of view and you can get answers about the services that you provide both positive and negative two and there is even a place to address any existing or growing complaints. That you take it seriously and also give the right answer while the customer is always right because the customer is a king.

You can also send customers cards and gifts to coincide with official events such as Ramadan and Hajj or on Christmas and New Year by taking into account your customers' events based on religious believes or customs, for example you are not expected to send a Christmas card to Muslim customer, or You do not need to send gifts or cards for Muslim holidays and events to none Muslim customer.

The strategy also helps you to have a well-skilled staff and management, and you also need to develop a business plan that links financial resources, brand values, customers, trademarks to supply partners and so on.

In order to benefit from the competitive advantage you have to create a new business product that is then more quality and less expensive than market price, and you always have in mind that you can lose customers and reduce your revenue, which you intend to keep improving all the time and not keep it in place.

 In order to expand your business and to make significant progress you must have a clear vision and strategy that defines the things we are talking about. If the top management clearly defines your business goals it can be a guide for the company's top executives and subordinates, and it can be a clear roadmap for success.

The team must decide strategy implementation can provide the opportunity to explore and bring strategy think about business opportunities as new businesses to open, so that to be achieved is to make assessment of business (marketing research) and research and information gathering and forecasting the business market and how it can best be developed.

8.5.1 Business Policy

Business policy is about how an organization is run or managed the business activity. This means that the management of the organization should pay attention to several different areas and should also coordinate those areas with each other.

Focusing on these supporting activities is aimed at realizing the goals and objectives of the organization. We set up areas according to the decision and ask for example only a few questions to answer the sector in the political process.

8.5.2 Personnel management.

This includes permanent and independent employees. You can even add a volunteer policy to this. Examples include questions such as: how do you give money to the people? What growth pathways can you provide for them? How will you strengthen the capabilities? How are responsibilities divided? How do you deal with writing or age pyramids?

Organization and cultural structure. How does the operation work internally? Which teams and jobs are needed? How can a culture of cooperation, feedback and quality assurance be maintained? How do you take care of internal communication?

8.5.3 The Finance.

This is about collecting and interpreting financial data using options that keep the organization healthy and safe for the future of the organization. How can you balance income and expenses in the long run? How can you differentiate and increase your sources of income? How can you and your directors keep track of the cash flows that work towards achieving strategic and operational objectives? How do you deal with making a backup?

8.5.4 Foreign Relations and PR.

How can you tell the organization and the operation? What is the possible relationship management for "customers" and stakeholders? How can you improve your relationships with the media or other forums?

Physical infrastructure: How can you manage your infrastructure on a regular basis? How can you best improve the impact? How can you create a better workplace for your employees? How do you organize traffic to and from the workplace?

8.5.5 Delivery of information and ICT.

How do you make sure your staff and volunteers get the information they need? How can you ensure robust ICT infrastructure? How do you support your people using ICT? How can you ensure effective knowledge management?

8.5.6 Quality assurance

In business operations, attention is paid to quality assurance. This is an active combination of ideas, techniques and methods, designed to maintain and improve the quality of activities and organization. Quality assurance is not a goal but a tool used by the agency, management and staff to ensure continuous improvement of results.

The choice of an organization of certain concepts, techniques and models of quality assurance is not an issue in itself. The important thing is that the organization can show that it is consciously and systematically engaged in quality monitoring and developing efforts to continually improve that quality.

8.6 Developing a Business Strategy

Rademakers (2018), As mentioned above the organization's business strategy requires that when making you obtained and made various studies which we have summarized in three:

1. Step One:

To determine the strategy of the business, 3 studies and analysis categories were set, namely:

1. To look at the quality, competence and knowledge of the top management of the company as CEO and subordinates. Determines the desired strategy and possible target
2. To monitor the quality of staff and their ability to handle new strategies, and to advise and support you in implementing the new strategy.

3. Consumers / customers and others associated with the organization or company it deals with. This requires them to enjoy and encourage them to have full confidence in the company.

4. to analyze the decision-making strategy in best away

1. How to make strategy:

I will explain below the key tips that will make it easier for you to develop a strategy; It is about the organization's communication with the outside and inside of your organization.

This is about how to prepare for dealing with the opportunities and threats that your organization or company may face.

Strategy also helps you build a good framework related to motivating activities and planning appropriate resources, defining objectives and how to implement them.

1. Review and predict threats and opportunities in the external environment. With the emergence of new companies in the market, there may be no failures at all, alternative products that can attract your customers, as well as assessing the purchasing power of your customers. The outside world offers new opportunities, new technologies and untapped potential markets. Ask yourself and find the answers to the following questions:

- What kind of financial system do we need to operate and how can that change?
- Are there any opportunities we can take advantage of?
- What are the risks associated with opportunities?
- Pay close attention to the inside of the company, look at your resources, your strengths and your performance. Be aware of the sources, your internal capabilities can make it difficult to choose your strategy, especially limited staff and limited resources.

So your strategy can only be effective if you get the support of the right sources and the right resources. Try to ask yourself the answers to the following questions:

What is our knowledge? How these are our competitive advantage?
- What are the sources that hinder or support our actions?
- Try to find ways to reduce the impact to address threats and to benefit the advantage and opportunities:
- Introduce many other new and undeveloped items. Often there is more than one single method of processing.
- Review all available facts, and ask all the questions to get the necessary answers related to the information you need.
- Scale and make sure you have complete information and do not miss important information to better evaluate a particular strategy, and then get the information.
- Choose and select the most talented people to lead the strategy (even if they are not in your team).
• 4. Do whatever it takes to improve and succeed in strategic support activities: Strategy is not just about customer success; it also involves a combination of chain link activities that your team and customers support together, as well as not being tied to your competitors. Your competitive advantage comes from the way things are connected and support and strengthen each other.

For example, if you work for or own an airline whose strategy is based on rapid change, which you can move to make a series of withdrawals and take full advantage of the
Aviation economy, this will affect Ticket prices can be reduced, which can be well taken advantage of by your customers, and these activities will help you achieve your goals.

• 5. Create alignment: Developing a strategy is the most important task
  Work planning and design, and is described as half of the work.

Other parts of the strategy are reinforced by the interconnectedness of the strategy, people and other activities of the company. What is important for each employee is:
1. Must be well aware of and understand the company's strategy
2. He must be aware of his role in the strategy

It is also important that they are consistent with other sources such as marketing and always keep an eye on the right customers, bonuses, real estate plans of the company. It must be in line with the organisation's behavior and strategy, and it must make the final decision on the organisation's senior management. It must be educated on how to adapt and implement it.

3.   Be ready to implement. Be prepared to focus and implement. In order to implement the strategy, it is necessary to find the implementers who, if necessary, have the necessary skills and capacity to run the project, provide the right tools, and design the financial resources required.

If the strategy is hopeless you should be prepared for:
- Understanding and recognizing bad news
- In order to quickly respond to do a review for the strategy.
Starting a business should be seen as a test, so if that test does not produce the desired result you are prepared to review it and change and adopt some parts of or altogether.

8.6. 1 Implementing a Business Strategy

Olsen(2020)According to Fortune magazine, an average of nine out of ten organizations fail to implement their strategic plan for a number of reasons:

- 60% of organizations are not linked to the new strategy in the company's budget
 - 75% of organisations do not include employee motivation when developing a new strategy.
  - 86% of business owners and senior executives spend less than an hour a month discussing or reviewing their new strategy.
   - 95% of regular employees in the organization do not fully understand the organization's strategy

Implementing a strategic plan requires another specific plan to be implemented. Each company or organization has its own way of implementing existing strategies. To implement your strategic is recommended to take the following steps:

1. Draw a strategic plan for the organization or companies first drafting the relevant people or groups, the owners or shareholders of the company to invest, then complete it after receiving all the recommendations and answers and then make a final copy.
2. Develop a budgeting plan using annual goals in line with financial assessments.
3. Make different plans that are appropriate for the different groups in the organization
4. Create a score cards format to check and monitor your plan.
5. Establish a system for monitoring performance and the structure of the reward system.
6. Submit your plan to the entire organization.
7. Develop departmental annual plans which is applying the corporate plan

8. Arrange monthly strategic meetings to get information on what has happened and what needs to be done.

9. Designate and prepare an annual strategic review date for the new evaluation holding large group meeting in the presence of all stakeholders, for the annual plan review.

10. Develop a plan of action for the coming year as well as a forecast for the coming year strategic plan.

9.10   Discussions Pros and cons on a local, national and international level

9.10.1 Business Strategy pros:

Clarity, you keep track of the direction and direction things are going. If you have a well prepared business strategy you should know where your business is at the moment, where it is going and what you inspired to get to where you plan to be in the future. This will help you to be clear and focus on the development of your business to achieve your goals.

1. Driving and accelerating your business and developing your business strategy will assist you and your team finding the right path and acceleration to grow your business.

2. A better understanding of where your business is going today. To grow and come up with a business strategy you need to know where your business is going right now. This has to do with understanding your business as a whole, including important internal factors such as financing, customer satisfaction, staff transfers, sales and marketing changes, conversion rates and so on.

3. You will also need to consider analyzing strength, weakness opportunities and threats related to business and understanding the business environment abroad, your competitors and the market you are in.

4. Long term contract for your business. Every time you build a business strategy you will decide on a long term plan and what you want your business to grow to get the most out of it. Suppose you want to take your profit x%, so that you can make your business more profitable and make a profit in the future.

5. Assess the key issues you want to do to achieve your planned strategy. Using and implementing your business strategy can help you identify the essentials and plans to grow your business where it stands today and where you would like it to be in the future. This is important for the implementation of your plan and business activities that are done on a daily basis.

6. Encourages discussion, discussion and consultation on business development and the adjustment and promotion of your business. You need to come up with a business strategy that everyone in the company will appreciate and welcome, and it is best to create a discussion within your experienced or senior team about where the business is going now, where it wants

to go and how to reach it. This debate can help to find a consensus strategy based on a common vision, and broad consensus, which can lead to the company's business objectives being achieved.

7.Creating new business opportunities. reorganised and reviewing your business strategy can lead to the creation of new business ideas that may not be as expected or unexpected.

8.Time to reflect and review your business. It can also give you time to re-evaluate your business and re-evaluate all parts and types of your business. At the same time, identify the current challenges facing your business. This can create momentum and encouragement for the company's employees who see themselves as important and have a stake in the company.

9.If you know and plan to go there, the strategy will make it easier for you to get where you want to be or where you want to be in order to be successful in your business.

10. Developing a business strategy plan can enable you to be more effective in business as you want to grow and develop your business with a specific goal you want to achieve, which you should pay attention to and waste time on strive to achieve your long-term business goals and objectives.

3.7.2 Cons: Business strategy:

On the negative side of business strategy there are differences of opinion, especially when the top business executives adopt an unrealistic strategy. It means someone who has created something beyond the scope or capacity of an organization or business that is not possible, which smells that customers doubt and do not believe or do not see that this can be beneficial and in the interest of the customer.

2. Failure to conduct a fact-based market study may result in your strategy not being based on facts and figures that are based on factual assumptions, and incorrect planning that may have a negative impact on your business.

3. If you do not consult with the people concerned about the strategy and do not listen to their side and how they see that the business can improve and develop its business, the poor business strategy could be impacted that you would not reach your desired goals.

4. If your policy and strategy is not based SMART (specific, measurable, achievable, realistic and time-bound) it may not be realistic and successful because you have not made a good assessment of the facts, and it will be difficult for you to implement it or may achieve the desired success.

5. If you have done the business plan or Strategic and financial resources and skilled labor to implement it does not matching in the plan of this could lead not your plan not to work properly or the plan could be failure as mission is impossible.

6. If you do not have a good knowledge of your position in the market, your strengths and weaknesses may also hinder you from achieving good results in your strategy.

7. If you do not get the official information and plans of your competing companies and their shortcomings and strengthening are not taken into account or underestimated it can be an obstacle to the implementation and fruition of the strategy you have developed.

8.8 Suggestion and Recommendations:

A policy plan provides an overview of how an organization conducts its work to achieve its goals. In terms of financial identification, a brief policy plan is sufficient. Depending on the size of your organization, social recognition requires a wide variety.

In general, you describe the business plans for the coming year, review them briefly and, if necessary, supplement a multi year plan. You should therefore update and republish your policy plans each year. On the following pages you will find a list of subjects that should in any case be included in a larger or smaller policy plan.

The strategy put out a value organization advocates. What did the organization want to achieve, how it wants to reach this and what is necessary to achieve this goal (people and resources).

You indicate that the focus of the organization in the coming years is emerging. What are the plans for the coming years? Policy is therefore understood to mean indicating the directions and the means by which the organization wants to achieve its objectives within the setting period.

To make proper business strategy of the company, you need to have a conference or a meeting of the company, which includes decisions from management team, business partner, or even anyone to company members so as to make discussion to have the appropriate strategy for the company for the coming year or coming years.

At such a meeting you can decide on the company's business strategy for the coming year after consulting and strategically planning and setting your goals.

If you want to achieve a goal, every stakeholder in the company should stand behind you and find out how you want to achieve your goals by consulting or listening to his or her opinion. If this is not the case, people can make up and tell unfounded stories and issues related to people's strategic activities and it will be difficult to achieve the goal everyone needs to know a reason and purpose to do their job. By planning what and how to give your people that reason.

If you feel that people are not doing what you expect, the first question to ask is, am I well-designed? and meet on your expectations. If the key people working with you are not satisfied with the strategy they are working on, their motivation may be too low which could hinder the success of the new strategy to be implemented.

1. Review and predict threats and opportunities in the external environment. With the emergence of new companies in the market, there may be no failures at all, alternative products that can attract your customers, as well as assessing the purchasing power of your customers.

2. Pay close attention to the inside of the company, look at your resources, your strengths and your performance. Be aware of the sources, your internal capabilities can make it difficult to choose your strategy, especially limited staff and limited resources.

3. Try to find ways to reduce the impact to address threats and to benefit the advantage and opportunities:
4. Introduce many other new and undeveloped items. Often there is more than one single method of processing.
5. Review all available facts, and ask all the questions to get the necessary answers related to the information you need.
6. Scale and make sure you have complete information and do not miss important information to better evaluate a particular strategy, and then get the information.

7. Ensure that Strategies to be based on SMART objectives (specific, measurable, achievable, (realistic (or relevant) and time-bound. The final company strategy is to be agreed upon by managers and staff to ensure that they are accepted and implemented and are ready to implement it).

8. Choose and select the most talented people to lead implementation and of the strategy (even if they are not in your team, you should hired them).
9. Do whatever it takes to improve and succeed in strategic support activities: Strategy is not just about customers success; it also involves a combination of chain link activities that your team and customers support together, as well as not being tied to your competitors. Your competitive advantage comes from the way things are connected and support and strengthen each other.

10. Create alignment: Developing a strategy is the most important task. Work planning and design, and is described as half of the work.

11. Be ready to implement. Be prepared to focus and implement. In order to implement the strategy, it is necessary to find the implementers who, if necessary, have the necessary skills and capacity to run the project, provide the right tools, and design the financial resources required.

12. Starting a business should be seen as a test, If the strategy not meet the desired target, necessary changes and adopt on time.

13. Ensures the integration and sustainability of the various segments of the business Strategy and competitive advantage. An organization has gained competitive advantage when it can meet the needs of its customers more efficiently and more efficiently than its competitors.

14. Consider bringing to market a products and services that customers are interested and value mostly.

15. Always keep in mind how to win a business competition as taking business competitive advantage leads to profitability, the strategy often focuses on ensuring that companies can gain and maintain a competitive advantage.

8.9 Conclusions

The strategy describes the ability of a company / organization to achieve its related goals to satisfy the needs of its customers, depending on how well the senior executives of the company perform their duties. The skills and leadership of senior management are critical to ensuring successful and successful efforts in the competitive capabilities of long-term companies.

The CEO of the company is responsible for the ultimate responsibility of managing the staff and managing the company's financial resources.

Strategies are important for companies because they enable them to gain value, gain value and strengthen their position in the market and make progress.

Creating a strategy allows the company to take progressive steps and increase the future performance of the company which can be seen in the performance, and the characteristics of the character, good which means to guide the company to lead the organization in the best way to achieve success.

In order to achieve its goals, the company must constantly adapt to the environment in which it operates. Competition is the evaluation of high-level economic conditions to evaluate the work done internally and externally.

The company's success is driven by the size and cost of the company. We sits in the company have strategy allows discovery of resources needed to compete with others, if the missing devices manages the company needs to carry out its activities, it is fair to reach the goal aiming.

Preferably through a review systematic, which allows managers and researchers to monitor the overall view of the system in accordance with the requirements to do strategy management of the company as it is appropriate to find a place to stay in the market as they know their place they stand in the market to then clarify where they want to go.

The strategy does not guarantee immediate success, but it does help organizations make important decisions in the long run. Rademakers (2018

Managers of all types of organizations should ask themselves the same 3 questions:

1. What is the current situation?
• Industrial and labor conditions
• Competitive position
• Company performance
• The strengths and weaknesses of the company

Active Actions to improve financial performance and gain competitive advantage Deliberate strategy (intentional strategy)
•Purposeful plans to build on previous decisions
•Responsive Provisional Response to Unexpected Developments and Emerging Market Strategies
•Adjustment strategic spontaneous, respond to changes in reaction
Instead of clear plans, experiment and experiment and the wrong process
Company performance
• The strengths and weaknesses of the company

2. Where do we want to go with the organization?
• Create the vision and goals of the organization
• Considering what new customers and stakeholders want

3. How will we get there?
• Explaining "who", "what" and "how" of the "action plan" strategy
• The most difficult and central aspect of this subject.
• Thinking about different things that will affect each other"How difficult is it to" beat people who fight."

As to response to changes in economic and market conditions and potential growth opportunities

.Manage business operations
Priority prioritizing resource allocation for activities that have the most impact on strategic performance Improve the organization's position on financial markets and support its financial performance Strategy = the general direction set by managers, competitive activities and business activities that they use to successfully compete, improve performance and grow the business.

• Great probability of success if the strategy differs from competitors and focuses on what others cannot or will not do
• Provides direction for the organization and tells them what to do and what not to do
• Ensures the integration and sustainability of the various segments of the business Strategy and competitive advantage
An organization has gained competitive advantage when it can meet the needs of its customers more efficiently and more efficiently than its competitors.
• Effectively on products and services that customers value highly
Very useful for one

• Since competitive advantage leads to profitability, the strategy often focuses on ensuring that companies can gain and maintain a sustainable competitive advantage
• Create lasting reasons for customers to choose the company over their competitors.

That is why the strategy should consist of items that are not readily available or quickly accepted by competitors. The strategy is about a different race than the competitor.

• Do what they did not do or better
• Do what they can't do o Do what differentiates an organization and attracts customers o Decide what to do and what not to do to gain competitive advantage Is competitive advantage sustainable in the 21st century?

Globalization creates "high level of competition" which also makes it impossible to maintain long-term profitability. Some scholars argues that the steady profits of competition cannot remain in many industries due to changes in technology, global marketing and legislation.

Therefore, it is better to look for "temporary benefits" the organization should make sure that it can quickly enter and exit the markets as soon as their competitors have a copy of their strategy.

if your company's strategy can be applied to another company, you don't have to be very good" of the constant benefit of competition, central to developing your strategy Strategic strategy will change over time.

Strategy involves making choices or options clearly related to how to compete and who and how to run it to achieve the required success.

There are only two benefits to competing: the ability to learn from customers as quickly as possible and the ability to turn the lessons learned into action faster than the competition. Business is a long game and the market is where the ball is, and the dance is between you and the other teams you are competing for. The team of the best players on the field plays well and the people follow and applaud.

Strategies are simplification and resource planning, and you should know that you cannot satisfy everyone, and you should always take into account the size of your business and your financial capacity.

Any company that wants to compete must know the best way to win and engage the minds of every employee.

Finally business strategy formulating and implementing is the process of tactics and plans to turn action and performance into a developed strategy and it is true that the implementation of your strategic plan precedes the development of the strategy.

Developing a policy and strategy is a simple task but it is very difficult and not easy to implement, which requires you to plan how to implement it and give it time to implement it otherwise there is no point in doing it and then putting it down. shelves, in order to ensure that they are made, a meeting should be held at least once a month, not once a week or two weeks.

8.9 Bibliography

Cukashmir(2020)https://www.cukashmir.ac.in/docs/MBA%20C%20402%20Unit%20II.pdf

MSG Content Team(2020) https://www.managementstudyguide.com/business-policy.htm

file:///C:/Users/User/AppData/Local/Temp/Samenvatting_1993_1588860496.pdf

https://www.hindawi.com/journals/je/2020/6253013/

Rademakers (2018), https://www.hindawi.com/journals/je/2020/6253013/

Chapter Nine

4. **Business Communication**.

9.11 Introduction to Business communication

I believe that every organization, whether commercial or non-commercial, needs to have a good business relationship within or outside the organization in which each organization must have a good relationship with its members and the surrounding defense in which it operates. .

The success or failure of an organization depends on its relationship with its customers and stakeholders, without which the business or service provided by the organization or company cannot function. I received the following subjects:

9.1.1 Objectives for Business Communication:

Commercemates(2018) explored the objectives of business communication and indicated the following objectives"

Communication is the medium through which wide information is exchanged within the business. It is simply a process of exchange of ideas, facts and information from one person to another person through a verbal or non-verbal medium

- Helps the company make the right decisions
- ensures that the business and services provided by the company run smoothly
- Creates an effective professional team that does the job well
- Increases customer engagement, which enables customer confidence and stakelhoders
- Increases productivity and reduces costs
- It develops and motivates the company's employees
- Facilitates the exchange of information related to the business and the service provided by the company.
- Enables the company to achieve its goals and objectives
- Provides leadership, mentoring and correction to those below them
- Enables and increases the production of effective products
- Improves employee morale and job satisfaction
- Enables the attraction of the company's customers and receives more offers than before which increases the company's revenue and profits
- Provides recognition of staff training needs, which in turn provides staff with the training and training they need.
- As a result, the company is making significant and visible progress.
It enhances the reputation and reputation of the company which enhances the overall image of the company or organization.

- Understand and demonstrate the use of basic and advanced business communication. techniques that today's technology demands, including anticipating audience reaction,
- Write effective and concise letters and memos,
- Prepare informal and formal reports,

- Proofread and edit copies of business correspondence.
- Use career skills that are needed to succeed, such as using ethical tools, working collaboratively, observing business etiquette, and resolving workplace conflicts,
- Plan successfully for and participate in meetings and conduct proper techniques in telephone usage,
- Use e-mail effectively and efficiently,
- Develop interpersonal skills that contribute to effective and satisfying personal, social and professional relationships, and
- Utilize electronic presentation software.

9.1.2 Definition:

Definition of communication is: intentional or unintentional (intentional or unconscious) to convey a specific message to another person. With one-way communication, the recipient may not respond immediately.

A company or corporation is a labor agency and active capital for the production and / or provision of goods and services. From a (ancient) economic point of view, companies focus on making a profit. A company that makes concrete products is also called a manufacturer.
A company can be described as an institution in which work and capital are central. Companies can be both commercial and non-commercial.

Business communication, is the process of managing, creating, communicating and building relations between the company and its environment, and it is the interpretation of ideas, facts, events, perspectives and feelings about the performance and development of the work, the effectiveness of organization and effectiveness as well as the goals of organizing and communicating.

The manager must be an active and effective journalist and no organization can succeed or develop, and an organization cannot build a good image and reputation without effective communication skills.

Poor communication systems can lead to mismanagement and unsatisfactory business results, or business failure.

The purpose of this essay is to show that the success of any business is to establish effective communication and that effective relationships are critical to the safety and development of business concerns. We also pointed out that communication skills need to be developed on a regular basis and especially in a business environment operating in a chaotic or unstable environment.

Communication is the sending of business messages to various media outlets; it can be conveyed in the form of verbal or non-verbal, formal or informal as long as it conveys an idea that evokes emotions, gestures, actions, etc. Good communication for business development is seen as a learned skill. Most people are born with a personal ability to speak, but we must speak fluently and choose the right words and phrases to communicate effectively.

It is also important when it comes to communication that you value other people who speak to you and that you listen carefully so that you understand what is being said and what the person is talking about, so that you can take advantage of it.

Speech, listening and our ability to understand the meaning of speech and speaking are skills we develop in different ways. We learn basic communication skills by looking at others and imitating our behavior based on what we see, for Communication is already the process of transferring, disseminating or passing information from one person to another or from one place to another.

In other words, communication is the process of creating, conveying and interpreting ideas, facts, ideas and emotions. It is a process basically shared by one, an exchange between two or more.

We receive training on basic communication skills to see how others are and focus on symptoms based on what we observed. It is important to note that the information is invaluable until it is made available to the person who needs it.

Communication is the process of distribution, disclosing, or transmitting information to one person to another or targeting more persons or audience. On the other hand it is the process of creating, reporting, conveying and interpreting theories based on facts, opinions and feelings.

It is basically a shared information process between two or more people. In addition, there is the exchange of information between directors/managers and their subordinates for the company.

9.12   Types of communication: Verbal, written, verbal and nonverbal

There are different types of communication within the science of communication. The four main ones are verbal communication, non-verbal communication, verbal communication and written communication.

When choosing between oral communication and text communication, it is important to consider the person (s) receiving the message. For example, if the sender chooses a written contact, he or she must make sure that everyone can read.

Verbal communication is associated with words. Non-verbal communication is communication without words, for example communicating with pictures or gestures, coordinates, shoulders, puzzles or laughter. Speech volume, speed, tone of voice, stress, thought accents and interactions are also subject to non-verbal communication.

Although they differ in verbal and non-verbal communication, they are connected in practice. The sender uses non-verbal communication to influence his purpose and message, for example to reinforce this. And the recipient also uses both verbal and non-verbal communication of the sender to translate the message.

Not only oral communication but also written communication consists of non-verbal aspects. For example, spelling, design and other features of the text speak to the characteristics of the channel.

Oral and written communication each has its own advantages and disadvantages. Oral communication is often fast, straightforward and personal, but also time dependent for text communication. The choice of these two forms of communication depends on the situation, the organization and the person. As a professional, you can often make this choice easily. But never choose a written form, because you find verbal communication too difficult.

9.13   General Analysis about the Business communication

Successful companies must have good communication skills to do their job. Consider, for example, marketing managers who force their leaders to convince them of their plans, organizational advisors who advise management and policy makers who force them to persuade their councils and board of directors of their proposals. These communication skills consist of written communication such as reports and oral communication, such as presentations.

The training showed that the best managers have excellent communication skills. This means that you have to be a communicative person, firstly, to have the opportunity to get a job and, secondly, to be successful in your job.

This chapter is limited to commercial communication, or formal communication. The formal communication comes from the transmission of the message from the sender to the recipient, in which the sender and / or recipient are connected to an organization. This organization may impose specific requirements on the communication system.

Commercial communication takes place in a number of places, including within business entities, in the non profit segment, but also in private life.

In the nonprofit section you will find this in the form of articles, articles, reports and circulars from the government. Private business communication occur when a person contacts an agency, for example in the form of a job application (letter), negative notice, statement or complaint.

We will focuses here on the most common types of business communication, which are practically carried out by almost everyone, such as letters, reports, speech proposals, conferences, discussions, etc. We will limit ourselves to human communication. Communication between computers or other devices so no action was taken.

Important symptoms
A business communication has several important characteristics:
1. It is always functional and is used to achieve the organizational goals on which it is based. (Example: a sales call is not only used to convince a consumer of product quality, but it should also lead to higher organizational change).
2. It does not usually occur in the name of a person, but is represented by an organization. Personal views are not discussed. Declares the position of the organization, taking into account the (company) structure of the organization as much as possible.
3. Most cases occur because an order has been given to do so. It is up to the contractor to carry out this task as much as possible. This means that the preliminary requirements set by the client must be taken into account, such as the length of the text, the last time it was held, the people involved, etc.
4. It is usually for different groups of readers, with different tastes, interests and interests (different target groups). This can lead to more articles or presentations. If this is not possible, one target group will have to be selected.
5. It should not take much time, especially for the recipients involved. To ensure this, the sender often has to spend the necessary time for communication, especially preparation, for example, a presentation or a meeting. However, it is his job and responsibility to make it as easy as possible for the recipien

Communication is of particular importance to the individual or group and the company or organization in which they work. In fact, communication with companies can be very rewarding and one can express one's thoughts through different means of communication.

Corporate communication is important and profitable. Improving and enhancing the exchange of information and communication with companies or others, you can benefit from understanding the relationship with other people or organizations, so by strengthening communication it is important to work with others.

In particular, it is not clear what everyone is doing. It is important to communicate well, both individually and as a group. It enhances when leaders are well aware of who is doing the work and that the staff is clear about the requirements for doing their job.

Assessmentinfo(2017), Most of companies provides training to anyone who wants to improve the quality of communication. They pay attention to the following points:
• analyze your communication culture, using feedback.

- handle different levels of communication
- deal with different reference circumstances
- increase listening and speaking skills
- Using questioning techniques, such as open and closed questions
- Have some kind of conversation

Share examples effectively
- Mirror. To communicate effectively, it is first important to present it in a mirror. During the training, camera recordings are used, so you can see for yourself how to communicate. For example, you may send in unstable and non-verbal signals, so that your communication does not go well. You can prevent this by learning to communicate effectively.

- Address deficiencies. In addition, it is important to learn how to deal with criticism. Are you always upset when someone working with you tells you something you don't agree with? When you learn to effectively communicate with, you will learn how best to respond it.

- Listen. It is also important to listen carefully. Communication is more than just sending a verbal and physical message to a companion. You are always a partner to talk to yourself and listen to what someone else has to say.

When you are too preoccupied with your ideas and pay close attention to what he has to say, you miss the message of the conversation and you yourself contribute to a useless communication goal by creating your distance when you are in a conversation you can watch and you can interpret it carefully.

Ways of communication to reach people
Much attention has also been given to the effective communication of communication science. American consultant Marty Brounstein, in his book Effective Communication of (Dummies, 2001), describes four general ways in which people communicate. The claim process seems to be good for effective communication.

The four phases are:
- Aggressive: We do not pay attention to the other person's feelings. Just communicate as you see fit, usually using the word "I". You don't seem to care how your communication partner understands your message, as long as they do what you ask them to do.

- Unprofessional: Although you would like someone to help you with something, you really do not dare to ask and go back and ultimately solve it yourself. Your communication goal has not been achieved this way.

- Aggressive Behavior: We do not dare to state your intentions in full. You often uses humorous metaphors to make explanation to show that any of you feel like you would like, however you solve the other person will feel a bit hurt and you deliberately appear to be the same size for yourself.

• Confidence system: Generally good method. Start with something positive and then move on to things that can improve. Encourage people to be kind by saying "I would love to ...", but also clarify: "Is it normal for us to meet later?"

9.14   Actualization how business communication topic applies to reality.

A business communication is a three-way communication between the sender or speaker, the recipient of the message to the audience and the message itself.

In order for the sender and receiver to understand each other, it is important that they listen to each other, that the sender speaks both clearly and intelligibly, and uses both verbal and non-verbal communication.

9.4.1 Effective communication:

A number of variables influence the effectiveness of communication. Some can be found in the environment in which communication takes place, some in the personalities of the sender and receiver, and others in the relationship that exists between sender and receiver. These different variables suggest some of the difficulties of communicating with understanding between two people.

The sender wants to formulate an idea and communicate it to the recipient. This desire to communicate may stem from his thoughts or feelings or may be caused by something in the environment. Communication can also be affected by the relationship between the sender and recipient, such as status differences, a staff-line relationship, or a student-teacher relationship.

Audience:
What the public needs to know
• How much do they know about the topic?
• What do they expect to see?
• What prejudices do they have or believe in?
• What is their agenda?

Sender:
What do you want her to tell and remember the audience?
• How you have shown that you are trustworthy and realible.
 • How do you show that you are in control of this place?
• What do you have in common with your audience to create a guarantee?

Message

• What are you trying to achieve?
- Inform or tell the public
- Satisfaction (that's always the case)
- Is your message needed?

NCSI(2011) Research has shown that the average employee receives about 190 messages per day via paper, voice mail, email, phone, etc. - from the Pitney-Bowes survey.

9.4.2 Types of communications:

1. The internal upward communication

Better business relationships are communications from employees under a manager or an individual reaching the hierarchy of organizations. A leader must be able to provide information and reports to increase the understanding of getting a serious looga service business.

Increased internal communication often includes surveys, feedback, forms and reports that employees submit to their managers or team leaders. For example, marketing information may include statistics such as the total number of website visitors, social media engagement, or total output generated.

2. The internal downward communication

The internal communication is from above or from one or more persons below. This type of communication can be in the form of a letter, a note or an oral will.

When talking to staff, leaders must maintain communication in a transparent and clean manner. Examples of such communications may include a statement of the company's new business practices, such as safety requirements and new regulations.

3. Internal lateral communication

Communication is thetrade between domestic workers in the workplace. Today there are many different ways employees can communicate: calls, messages, emails, solutions for employee communication programs.

This type of communication can take place within departments and is more common than other types of business communication. In addition, regular communication with staff plays an important role in employee engagement and productivity.

4. External relations

A foreign business relationship is any relationship that takes place in external parties such as customers, prospects, vendors or partners. Unlike all forms of business communication within the country, external communication takes place regularly.

Smarp(2019) Surveys show that 80% of workplace problems are related to poor organizational communication. In order to solve this problem, communication within the organization must be strengthened and senior staff should be able to provide relevant and important information to the workforce. In addition, staff members to report and sharing the important news to the superiors.

9.5 Componants of communication

The communication system involves understanding, sharing, and meaning, and consists of eight key elements related to the discussion of non-personal communication issues with business-related issues: source, message, channel, receiver, feedback, environment, context, and interference

In order to better understand the communication process, we can break it down into a series of eight essential components:

1. Source
2. Message
3. Channel
4. Receiver
5. Feedback
6. Environment
7. Context
8. Interference

Each of these eight components serves an integral function in the overall process. Let's explore them one by one.

Source

The source imagines, creates, and sends the message. The source begins by first determining the message—what to say and how to say it.

The second step involves encoding the message by choosing just the right order or the perfect words to convey the intended meaning.

The third step is to present or send the information to the receiver or audience. This message can be conveyed through his or her tone of voice, body language, and choice of clothing.

Finally, by watching for the audience's reaction, the source perceives how well they received the message and responds with clarification or supporting information.

Message

The message is the meaning produced by the source for the receiver or audience. When you speak to a person your message may be the words you choose that will convey your meaning. But that is just the beginning. The words are brought together with grammar and organization. You may choose to save your most important point for last.

The message also consists of the way you say it—in a speech, with your tone of voice, your body language, and your appearance—and in a report, with your writing style, punctuation, and the headings and formatting you choose. In addition, part of the message may be the environment or context you present it in and the noise that might make your message hard to hear or see.

Imagine, for example, that you are presenting in front of your class and are aware there is the Super Bowl game tonight. Your audience might have a hard time settling down, but you may choose to open with, "I understand there is an important game tonight." In this way, by expressing verbally something that most people in your audience are aware of and interested in, you might grasp and focus their attention.

Channel

There are different ways for a message to travel between the source and the receiver and this is called the channel. For example, think of your television. How many channels do you have on your television? Each channel takes up some space, even in a digital world, in the cable or in the signal that brings the message of each channel to your home. Television combines an audio signal you hear with a visual signal you see. Together they convey the message to the receiver or audience.

Turn off the volume on your television. Can you still understand what is happening? Many times you can, because the body language conveys part of the message of the show. Now turn up the volume but turn around so that you cannot see the television. You can still hear the dialogue and follow the story line.

Similarly, when you speak or write, you are using a channel to convey your message. Spoken channels include face-to-face conversations, speeches, telephone conversations and voice mail messages, radio, public address systems, and voice over Internet protocol (VoIP). Written channels include letters, memorandums, purchase orders, invoices, newspaper and magazine articles, blogs, e-mail, text messages, tweets, and so forth.

Receiver (Recipient)

As a recipient you listen, see, touch, smell, and / taste to get a message and interpret the message from the source tentionally and intentionally. To better understand this section, think about the football team's pick-up kit. The circular throws the ball to the courier, who must see and interpret where the ball is being held. The delay may be intended for the recipient to "catch" his message in one form, but the recipient may see things differently and miss the football (meaning) altogether.

Feedback

When you reply to the sender, intentionally or unintentionally, you are responding to a message related to the message. Feedback consists of messages that the recipient returns to the source or sender. Verbally or verbally, all of these feedback signals enable the eye to see how best, correctly (or negatively and incorrectly) a message is received.

Feedback also gives the recipient or audience an opportunity to ask for evidence, to accept or reject it, or to show that the source can make the message interesting. As the response rate increases, communication accuracy also increases.

For example, suppose you are on the ground floor of your home with your children upstairs. You would like to tell her that dinner is ready. So the question is how do you convey it or do you shout at them from above so that they can come down and hear the message and react..

9. Pros and cons on Business and communication

9.6.1 Pros:

Gaile, B(2015) Have you ever noticed how some of the staff or some teams within the work environment seems to be isolated or distant from others? There is one person or group that does not seem to know others.

This makes it difficult to know where they work and what they produce, how much their work is valued, or it is difficult to decide whether their products are beneficial to the overall mission of the company. This can then be a solution to establishing a communication system that is accountable. The workplace is no benefit in pattern open communication, and this well thinking about them. Below I summarize the pros and cons of workplace communication.

1. It opens up more opportunities for creativity to move forward.

Humans are a complex animal with great stories to tell. The experiences we have together are unique to ourselves. There is really no one in the world like us. It is this personal level that inspires creativity in many different ways. If there is enough communication in the workplace, this creativity can be sent where it is needed, to get the job done.

2. It closes the distance between two people or groups.
Conversations can eventually put one person or group in someone else's shoes, even if it is for a short time. This allows each party to communicate with a perspective outside of them selves.

The information gathered from such experiences can then deepen personal perceptions as it brings people together.

3.   Workplace communication can encourage creativity.

The special thing about human communication is that it transmits information. They are like a sponge, and smokes a small amount of data and the impact those around them every day. This information can only be passed from person to person, but it can be passed down from generation to generation. Workplace communication can encourage creativity as new eyes can see gaps in information that others may not see.

4. It happens quickly and requires little investment time.
In the past, it was almost necessary for remote groups to work independently due to relationship restrictions. These restrictions no longer exist. If it is possible to talk in real time to a half-world office, then it is possible to talk to staff sitting at three tables below to get their views. Many of the restrictions imposed on communications today are self-imposed.

9.6.2 What are the cons of communicating in the workplace:

1. Sometimes communication can be deceptive

The real issue at work is that there are political issues going on there. This can make it harder when we get together, it can also cause when a group of people get together, and people can meet in a place where everyone can feel comfortable talking. If one group wants to meet with another group to benefit from it. In that case, the relationship between the two groups could be to the advantage of the other party and to the detriment of the other party. To avoid this business communication in the workplace to be based win-win policy.

2. It can tear people apart

Communication is a double-edged sword, it can help people get together or meet, but it can also increase and widen the gap between them. There is such a thing as honesty. Telling someone that they are stupid or useless or, unprofessional employees, and it may be true what you are saying, but it does not help to motivate and motivate that person to be productive and very effective.

 If we are not careful in terms of saying we want to give a feed back and not well chosen statement saying workers at the workplace, so people can hate alignment and distance between them. Then try to feed the person you are feeding back to about not hurting his or her feelings and not saying harsh words that make him or her feel angry or demeaning.

3.   **It creates too much connectivity at times.**

Some workplace communication is a good thing. With modern technology, however, many employees are connected to each other. There is no place for anyone to escape or hide until he decides to open up and escape from his workplace network. When that happens, they may find peace, confidence and love, but also they can lose communication occurs while they are outside of work are missing, creating future losses.

In some ways, too high a connection is a situation that cannot always be overcome. It is good for employees to be connected and have a professional relationship and focus on the work and how to complete it during the work, but it is not given priority to be a very close friend and if they disagree in the future each has personal stories and his friend's faults. the work he puts out. This can have a devastating effect on the job.

4.   Communication can be difficult to decipher at times.

Communication can happen quickly in a day at work, but that does not mean that a complete understanding has been reached through the emerging information. Communication in the workplace today can be limited and fast, making it difficult to know what is being said or what the goals are. This makes communication easier because there is a lot of effort to connect with each other today.

The advantages and disadvantages of communication in the workplace show that sometimes there can be many good things. Communication must be effective, accurate, and meaningful. When that happens, there is no limit to the stories that can be told.

Also, if there is interest related to the workplace, it is appropriate to formal inform employees of the information and correct their leaders, to looga prevent information incomplete or the fact that in the country to get the staff that everyone can rely on the translation and details it wants.

Communication problems arise when:
• Code messages do not meet the five criteria stated;
• The sender pursues unclear goals.

Without a clear purpose in mind, it is impossible to make a good message and write it correctly. If you do not know your purpose, you cannot collect information, select information or choose a type, color or format.

• The message does not (appropriately) match the sender's goals.

This happens when the sender has a clear goal in mind, but is unable to create a communication message. The sender then does not know what to expect from him.
It is also possible that the sender's intent was already clear, because the message is not enough to "cover".

This can be a problem when the sender wants to be satisfied because the recipient does not know he can be satisfied. Messages aimed at convincing the recipient should therefore obscure the recipient's view of that purpose.

• Messages or goals do not meet the needs of the recipient.
 Example: promoting a particular product is only effective if there are people (possibly) interested in the product. If no one is interested in the product, it makes no sense to advertise.

• The code does not match the sender's goals, so the recipient does not interpret the message correctly.

• Settlement or mediation does not meet the needs of the recipient.
Example: A newly opened store has chosen to contact all residents in the area by phone, while these residents prefer to be notified in writing to the store. For example, through paper or envelope.

4.7 Recommendations and suggestions

The internal communication of the companies is important for each organization to work well to strengthen the communication of the members of the organization. It is important that the members of the organization can easily communicate with the team members they work with as well as the senior management, which can help the team achieve their goals of increasing productivity and revenue of the company.

The following is a summary of important steps to strengthen the organization's internal communication:

 The following list includes practical steps to improve internal communication:

     1. Make organization information easily accessible.

Smarp(2020), It points to a survey of 4 out of 5 employees who believe that effective internal business communication helps them to be more efficient and successful in their work.

It is said that on average, employees spend 2.5 hours a day searching for information related to work, to prevent so many security checkpoints that time, it is important that workers can quickly find the information they need and there is a political system has available.

In addition, the average worker spends 2.5 hours a day searching for the required information. Each month, these results are a week's worth of time to find something that should include fingerprinting staff.

Each organization has its own internal knowledge, or "sticky" information, that all employees understand. It is not easy to easily understand how an organization operates, and it can take a long time to understand. To address this, it is important to educate and train staff on how the organization works and how internal information and documents are used as a reference.

2. Make goals and objectives clear:

You need to explain the values and goals, and include them in the training of company employees. This can make it easier for employees to better understand the purpose and goals of the company to promote communication and social cohesion.

3.Strengthening Relationships

When it comes to relationships between team members working not only within the company, but also in the relationship between company executives and subordinates.

In order to achieve this, the management of the company must ensure that the internal relations of the companies are trained by the employees. It is also important that managers spend time with their employees and get to know each other better and listen to the opinions and feedback of their employees.

Managers should not listen to and understand the concerns and grievances of their employees, so that employees feel important and listened to and their personal and group concerns are addressed, which can lead to the company losing the trust of its subordinates.

4.Create an Open Dialogue

It is also important for executives to be informed of new developments and changes being made by the company.

This can be achieved, for example, with a two-month newsletter or regular company meetings. It is also a good idea for staff to take part in the discussion and ask their bosses questions.

Keep employees informed of company changes, developments and future plans. This can come in a bi-monthly newsletter or company meetings. In addition, allow staff to participate in this discussion. Encourage questions and comments, and show that all ideas are welcome. Employees are more likely to communicate well when they feel they have a stake in where the company is headed.

5.Promoting Information Sharing

Employees need to have an online platform for the exchange of information and knowledge. It is important for employees to have a consistent reading attitude so that they can continue to exchange important information about their work and that employees can receive direct updates increase in relation to their work for the company or organization.

Employees should have access to a forum or platform where information and updates can be provided so that employees can keep up to date with any new developments at any time.

This can provide staff with an opportunity to keep track of progress and changes in the workplace, and help them keep abreast of the progress of the ongoing project and progress.

Not to be outdone by employees and their bosses face-to-face, but the online platform further enhances the conversations and interactions that employees can use even when they are not at work and on leave from work.

9.8 Conclusions

Communication is one of the most important aspects of the business world. Professional men and women use communication for getting ahead, resolving interpersonal conflicts and working collaboratively with others to achieve unified goals. Since communication is such a necessary business component, business people must familiarize themselves with communication techniques that will be most effective for them and their professional counterparts.

While communication comes easily to people in many situations, in the workplace it's often a different story. Business settings require special considerations when it comes to communicating effectively, especially during times of conflict. If you feel like your communication skills aren't up to par, don't worry; with a little practice, positive communication skills can be learned.

Bianca, A(2020) Business owners and employees with excellent communication skills can effectively contribute to a workplace culture and have a greater impact on customers. Communication skills are important when collaborating on projects, providing service to customers, sharing ideas in training sessions and participating in other diverse business situations.

People who can send and receive messages clearly serve as representatives of a company's brand and are more effective in their jobs. Communication is essential for everyone in a company. Communication offers employees and managers alike the opportunity to express concerns and ideas in the workplace.

An employee who lacks communication skills can become frustrated with co-workers, workplace rules and managers because his ideas and concerns aren't heard. Coaching an employee to communicate better requires a manager to invest time to personally sit down one-on-one with the employee and explain what communication consists of.

Business communication, we can say is anything related to the business or service relationship of a company or organization. Entrepreneurs are made up of different people living in different places working in different business ventures.

Or people who work together in an organization or company with clear goals and objectives that they want to achieve in the future. Look at your organization's customer service staffs who answers the phone, the customers you serve and other business relationships between the company and other stakeholders including the customer or other companies that have a close business relationship. They are all an important part of the business. Effective business communication depends on the structure of the company or organization and its leadership.

A business relationship is sending and receiving messages and replying to messages within a company, organization or business. Business communications include verbal, non-verbal, public and cultural communication to promote employee retention, customer satisfaction and a healthy business relationship with the company.

Purpose

The purpose of business communication is to strengthen and enhance, educate and develop relationships, in order to gain trust and positive social recognition. When business communication is achieved correctly, the result will be success because it focuses on communication and caring for people.

Types of business relationships - Top / Bottom

Martic(2020), Business relationships run in one of two ways: up or down. Increasing communication is messages sent from people under senior management. Increased communication is feedback, reports and development meetings to inform the management of their organizations' effectiveness.

Communication decreases when a message is sent from someone higher than the one below. For example, if the executives of Dahabshil Company, the largest company in Somaliland, send a message to the chairman of Dahabshiil Company, the telecommunications company is considered to have gone to the top management of the company, and when the management responds to that message it will be subordinate to the other management, company under the top leadership.

166

Challenges

Business relationships can be limited or prevented by the shared barriers of communication. Barriers to business communication can distort the message or prevent one from understanding its meaning states that the most common barriers to business communication are: distracting environment, poor message structure, misinterpreted message delivery, weak delivery, mixed message and misuse of media.

Considerations

Business communication is an ever-evolving process that thrives on evaluation, observation and implementation of needed change. Conducting an organization's needs assessment will give the business an overview of the effectiveness of the company's communication. Leaders should seek out communications professionals to increase the knowledge of leaders and managers. It identifies areas of weakness and provides advice on how to improve those areas.

Trust begins with honest, communication and personal relationships. Is it possible to improve your personal relationship? How do you work with a real relationship, can you be good at building relationships or gaining confidence in the past?

If yes, how do you do that and where does this development begin? Proper manners, clear intentions and awareness of your character are the first steps on the path to a positive and trusting relationship. Everyone can improve their communication skills and make their relationship more effective and Communicate effectively.

Duits(2020), With effective training and consulting you will clearly learn how to be successful in communication, customer engagement, presentation and advice. To get you started on good communication today, here are 10 tips to improve your overall communication skills;

1 Always start your conversation with a positive "mind"

2 Try to be direct in your communication, without too much unnecessary writing

3 Observe non-verbal communication (behavior)

4   Ask questions and identify the questions you want to ask

   5.   Do not distract (phone, thought!)

6.Get ready

7.Try the other place now and then

8.Keep your goal in mind

9.Some times ask "how can I help you?"

10   Earn to listen carefully (truth and honesty!)

9.9 Refrences

Assessmentinfo (2020), retrieved 05-12-2020,online access:
https://www.assessmentinfo.nl/effectiefcommuniceren/

Gaile, B(2015) , Pros and cons of communication, retrieved 13-12-2020),available online:
https://brandongaille.com/8-pros-and-cons-of-communication-in-the-workplace/

Kristina Martic(2020), 11 reasons why business communication is crucial for company
success.https://blog.smarp.com/11-reasons-why-business-communication-is-crucial-for-companys-success

Duits(2020), verbeter zakelijke communicatie, https://kweekel.nl/kweekel-magazine/verbeter-zakelijke-communicatie-begin-vandaag-10-tips/

Mallory Otis(2020) How to Build Positive Communication Skills, Copyright 2020 Hearst
Newspapers, LLC, retrieved 23/12/2020,**https://smallbusiness.chron.com/build-positive-communication-skills-10477.html**

**Commercemates(2018))objectives of communication,retrieved on 26-12-2020,online avaible:
https://commercemates.com/purpose-communication/**

Wikipedia(2020),   Business communication. retrieved 12-12-2020
https://en.wikipedia.org/wiki/Business_communication#Methods_of_business_communication

Van Jansen(2013), Samenvatting Zakelijke communicatie, retrieved 24-12-2020https://www.worldsupporter.org/en/chapter/38735-samenvatting-zakelijke-communicatie-1-van-janssen

NCSL (2011), Communication, retrieved on 10-12-2020, accessonline
https://www.ncsl.org/documents/NLSSA/Communication_NLSSA_2011.pdf

Printed in Great Britain
by Amazon

86530564R10099